HAMLET:
AN HISTORICAL AND COMPARATIVE STUDY

BY

ELMER EDGAR STOLL, Ph.D.

GORDIAN PRESS
NEW YORK
1968

Originally Published 1919
Reprinted 1968

AAX3306

Library of Congress Catalog Card Number 67-30880

Published by Gordian Press, Inc.

CONTENTS

The more I read him, the more I am convinced that as he knew his own particular Talent well, he study'd more to work up great and moving Circumstances to place his chief Characters in, so as to affect our Passions strongly, he apply'd himself more to This than he did to the Means or Methods whereby he brought his Characters into those Circumstances.—*Some Remarks on the Tragedy of Hamlet* (1736), p. 55.

It may be safely asserted that the simpler explanations are, and the less they are biased by the subtleties of the philosophical critics, the more likely they are to be in unison with the intentions of the author.—Halliwell-Phillips, *Memoranda on the Tragedy of Hamlet* (1879), p. 13.

But for all that he or Hamlet has got by it [*i.e.*, the dramatist's effort to avoid the impression of a weakness in him], Shakespeare might too evidently have spared his pains, and for all this voice [*i.e.*, Swinburne's own] as of one crying in a wilderness, Hamlet will too surely remain to the majority of students, not less than to all actors and all editors and all critics, the standing type and embodied emblem of irresolution, half-heartedness, and doubt.—Swinburne, *A Study of Shakespeare* (1879).

HAMLET[1]

CHAPTER I

DIFFICULTIES, AND ONCE NO DIFFICULTIES

It is in humility of spirit that one must, in these latter days, approach *Hamlet*, pen in hand. How many pens have touched it, and the riddle still unread! A German critic, who for the moment spoke as if he had somehow got on the wrong side of the Rhine, once said that in every essay on *Hamlet* there are two parts, a good and a bad: the good being the part in which the author confutes all previous theories; the bad, the part in which he produces a theory of his own. It is almost wholly the bad, then, that I have now to offer, for with previous theories I shall deal only as they stand directly in the way.[2] Two excuses I have for so doing. As for the one, paper, nowadays, and your printer's and your reader's time are precious; as for the other, the purpose that I set before me is not the ordinary one. It is to discover, if possible, something of the dramatist's intention. Many other students, no doubt, have had the same purpose, though they have generally proceeded as if their purpose were another and the play were written yesterday. Many have directly or indirectly confessed that the dramatist's intention did not matter to them at all. In doing so they fly in the face of venerable precept,—though not of practice, to be sure, whether in this or in any day:

> In every work regard the writer's end.

> A perfect judge will read each work of wit
> With the same spirit that its author writ.

It is in two ways that I undertake to ascertain this spirit, to discover this end. One is by studying the technique, construction, situations, characters, and sentiments of the play in the light of other plays in which similar construction, situations, characters, and sentiments appear. It is thus, ever since George Steevens made the suggestion, that philologists have proceeded in the study of Shakespeare's language. They arrive at the meaning of old phrases by comparing them with the same or similar ones elsewhere in Shakespeare or in other Elizabethan books. The method is equally necessary for the understanding of his technique and ideas, though it has been but little used. If the meaning of the lesser

---

[1] In this little monograph are to be found some views presented in my article on *Hamlet* in the *Kittredge Anniversary Papers*, though generally much modified and altered. From the article I sometimes quote—without quotation marks,—but otherwise, save in one reference, I ignore it. In part, and in simpler form, the present piece of writing was read in April, 1917, as a public lecture at Stanford University. A forthcoming monograph on the *"Problem of Hamlet"* by the Right Hon. J. M. Robertson is announced in the *Times* as I go to press.

[2] For a review of the principal theories, and an estimate of them in which I concur, I beg to refer the reader to Professor Bradley's *Shakespearean Tragedy* (1908), pp. 94-108.

element of expression be the property of the past, surely the meaning of the larger is not the possession of the present. Technique and ideas change as well as words, and sometimes faster; and these are the changes that have done 'most to becloud the author's meaning and lead his readers astray.

The other way of discovering the dramatist's intention is by studying the modifications which Shakespeare made in his material. "Not why did it happen, but how did it happen," said Goethe, "is the scientific question." It is a prime critical question, some scholars think, as well. So recent a drama as Goethe's *Faust* is not to be understood until we know the sources, the texts and the revisions, the early passages and the late, and the influences which determined and moulded these. Only then can we begin to answer the question *wherefore*, and perceive the dramatist's purpose winding through. And of still greater moment are such considerations of origin and development in the criticism of *Hamlet*. No more than Goethe's poem did *Hamlet* spring out of the author's brain like Minerva out of Jupiter's, full-grown. He did not write a play but rewrote one; and not once but twice at least did he rewrite it—first, in the version of Quarto 1,[3] and, second, in the version of Quarto 2 and the Folio.[4] And it is as we compare these, and then confront them with what we can make out of the old play on Hamlet, now lost to us, that we begin to perceive the dramatist's purpose here. Though this course, like the other that I have described, has been followed by students before me, it has not been followed to the end of the road. And by nearly all of them it has been followed in the light of a different hypothesis. They have

[3] I have tried to avoid taking up my position on doubtful or disputed ground. For this reason I have avoided letting anything hinge on the *Fratricide Punished* (see below, p. 4, notes). But as for Quarto 1, I must premise that it represents the first of two Shakespearean versions. That is, it is not to be explained merely as Shakespeare's single and final version mutilated in the reporting, and interpolated by a third party who is neither Shakespeare nor the original author. In doing so I am but following the opinion of the Cambridge editors, an opinion which, I think, generally prevails. Professor Creizenach and his followers may succeed fairly well with their interpolation theory until it comes to the structure of the play. Here it breaks down. There was mutilation in the reporting, of course; there may have been interpolation by a third poet, though how that is to be ascertained I cannot see; but neither process at all explains such matters as the presence of the nunnery scene, with the "To be or not to be" soliloquy, in Act II instead of Act III, or the absence of the last soliloquy of Quarto 2, together with the remarks about hoisting with the petar and the pirate capture, which depend upon it, or the present form of the closet scene. (See below pp. 28 ff.) It is simply turning history upside down to make all the primitive touches and simpler structure in Quarto 1 subsequent to the version of Quarto 2. (See below, p. 36, note 13, for evidence that the original position of the nunnery scene, with the "To be or not to be" soliloquy, was where it stands in Quarto 1.) And I am pleased that the latest bibliographical evidence, on which I light at the last moment, is on this side. See Mr. J. D. Wilson, *Library*, July, 1918, pp. 168-9.

Professor Creizenach is a great authority, who commands the respect of every student. But his tendency is, whenever possible, to consider an Elizabethan play with the same plot as one of Shakespeare's a corruption of Shakespeare's. He seems nobly jealous for the poet's reputation. But surely he went far astray in making the *Taming of a Shrew* subsequent to the *Taming of the Shrew*; he went equally far astray, I think, with his similar theory as to Quarto 1 and the *Fratricide Punished* (see below, p. 4, note 10).

[4] The Folio version was the acting version—Quarto 2 somewhat abridged. With it I do not much concern myself in this monograph.

sought for something different—and is it not one of life's ironies that of truth, if not of happiness, what we seek we find? They have found in the modifications evidence of a purpose psychological[5] rather than dramatic.

1

What Shakespeare in the first place undertook was to rewrite the lost old play (probably composed about 1588) for the Lord Chamberlain's Servants in 1601 or 1602.[6] There are many reasons for thinking that the old play was by Thomas Kyd; there are no reasons for thinking it was by any one else; but it was in any case a play very similar, both in plot and in style, to Kyd's other revenge play, the *Spanish Tragedy*.[7] Now the Kydian revenge play had recently come back into favor. Ben Jonson had just penned "additions" to the *Spanish Tragedy* for Henslowe's rival company, the Children at the Blackfriars; and the Lord Chamberlain's Company at the Globe must needs have something like it to keep even. And who so fit for this as Shakespeare, their chief poet, who, in *Titus Andronicus*, years before, had beaten Kyd at his own game? Neither Shakespeare nor Jonson, we may presume, was expected to make the story over. Kyd's two plays had been universally popular;[8] and what the company—what the public—wanted was *Hamlet* or the *Spanish Tragedy*, nothing less. Dramatic art in those days moved apace—hence the rewriting; but what the company desired, and what the public which was attached to an old play would relish, was not new matter but new

[5] This is true in some measure even of Professor Lewis's *Genesis of Hamlet*, a little book which has received both high praise and severe censure, but deserves, I think, only the former. My indebtedness to it here and there is conspicuous, although I arrive at different conclusions.

[6] This date is compatible, as it seems, with Gabriel Harvey's allusion to *Hamlet* in the margin of his Speght's Chaucer, which inclines Professor G. C. Moore Smith (*Harvey's Marginalia*) to a date of 1598. The reference to the Earl of Essex implies, as Professor Moore Smith observes, that he is still alive, and he died in February, 1601. And the inclusion of Shakespeare among "our flourishing metricians" implies, as Professor Boas observes, that Harvey was here concerned with *Hamlet* not as a stage play but as a piece of literature. *Hamlet* did not appear in print till 1603, but Harvey might have seen the manuscript. In any case, the date 1598, which, along with his name, he placed on the title page, and also on the last page of the book, means no more than a librarian's stamp. The "Gabrielis harveij, et amicorum, 1598," which he put at the end does not mean that he ended reading the book in 1598, but that he marked it at the beginning and at the end when he bought it. The note on *Hamlet*, moreover, is not at the end of the book, but at f. 394 *v.*, about twenty pages back, after the text and before the list of "hard words." There is no connection, therefore, between note and date.

Whether Shakespeare's first revision, ill represented in Quarto 1, goes back, as Messrs. Wilson and Pollard would have it, to 1593, does not concern us here. See their interesting communications in the *Library*, June, 1918, and *Times Literary Supplement*, Jan. 9-16, 1919, both of which reach my hands as I go to press.

[7] I take Kyd's authorship for granted, but it is not indispensable to my argument. Kyd's authorship seems as definitely settled as a literary question can well be; but it is possible, though not probable, that some other playwright dominated Kyd, or was dominated by him, to the point of their making plays so similar.

[8] There has, in one quarter, been the opinion that the old *Hamlet* was not so popular as the *Spanish Tragedy*. But the allusions up to the appearance of Shakespeare's version seem to be even more numerous, and the influence of the story on the stage more profound. Marston's revenge plays as well as Tourneur's are imitations of it rather than of the *Spanish Tragedy*; indeed the *Spanish Tragedy* itself is the Hamlet story transposed, and was written no doubt in expectation of a like success.

form,—crudities in construction, situation, and sentiment softened down, and word and verse wakened to life by the most magical of pens. The story, the telling situations, the essential conception of the characters,— these they could not easily surrender. Indeed, the great popular artist, such as was Shakespeare, in sympathy with his public and their likings and cravings, would himself not desire that they should surrender them. He was not the one to risk disappointing an audience assembled to witness a familiar and favorite performance on the stage and applaud a popular hero. Rather, he would run to meet their prepossessions and predilections. He always followed the tradition of the stage, he never ignored it or defied it. Richard III, Falstaff, Prince Hal, are cases in point. Whether he knew it or not he followed the Horatian precept:

> Sit Medea ferox invictaque, flebilis Ino,
> Perfidus Ixion, Io vaga, tristis Orestes.

And this presumption is supported by the evidence. From a comparison of our *Hamlet*, in its three Shakespearean texts, with the *Spanish Tragedy*, which is powerfully influenced by the old *Hamlet*, with the *Bestrafte Brudermord* (or *Fratricide Punished*, as we shall call it), the seventeenth-century German play based upon the old *Hamlet*,[9] and with Belleforest's novel, the ultimate source of all,—from a comparison of our play with all these, I say, most scholars have come to the conclusion that in plot, in incident, and in the outlines of the characters, Shakespeare's *Hamlet* was not greatly different from Kyd's. In Kyd, too, to speak summarily, there was the secret adultery, the secret murder, and the Ghost to reveal them to the son; feigned madness, delay, and self-reproaches; a series of attempts to discover the cause of Hamlet's madness, conducted by the King; the play-within-the-play and the sparing of the King at prayer; the scene in the bedchamber between the Prince and his mother, and the murder of the eaves-dropping counsellor; the voyage to England, with some stirring adventures on the way; the madness and the suicide of Ophelia; the fencing-scene, with poison on the foils and in the bowl; and vengeance snatched by the hero only after he himself at last is caught in the clutches of death.[10] Matters of plot these are in the main, but how

---

[9] That it is based on the old *Hamlet* is the opinion, it would seem, of the majority of sound scholars —among the recent ones, MacCallum, Thorndike, Evans, Schick—though there are names so eminent as Creizenach's against it. But since it is still a matter of dispute, I have tried to let nothing in the subsequent argument hinge upon it alone. The play as preserved belongs to the year 1710, but it may of course be much older. A *Tragoedia von Hamlet* was acted in Dresden in 1626. The fullest recent discussion of its relation to Kyd and Shakespeare and Belleforest is that of Professor M. B. Evans, *Der Bestrafte Brudermord* (Litzmann's *Theatergeschichtliche Forschungen*, 1910).

[10] Professor Creizenach, who is jealous for the great poet's reputation, declines to cede the tragic ending to Kyd. This is in keeping, of course, with his refusal to find much of Kyd in Quarto 1 anywhere, or to admit that the *Fratricide Punished* is derived from the original *Hamlet*. However it be, there is the very similar tragic ending, death huddled upon death, in the *Spanish Tragedy*. In both, in highly theatrical fashion, the hero himself falls as he attains his revenge. As in Hieronimo's play-within-the-play, so in the final episode of the fencing-match between Hamlet and Laertes, when (as the stage-

far Shakespeare preserves the traditional character of the hero we are yet to see.

It thus appears that two great improbabilities in the play as we have it lay embedded in the story when Shakespeare took it over.[11] One is that the hero should undertake to feign madness in the presence of the murderer and thereby alarm him in his secret guilt. In Belleforest the fact of the fratricide was known and acknowledged; and madness was feigned, as in the case of David when in Gath and of Brutus when menaced by Tarquin, almost wholly for self-protection. Kyd, by making the murder secret and introducing the Ghost to divulge it, at once did away with the reason for feigning madness at all. Instead of protecting the revenger, it now alarmed the murderer. The other improbability (and a far greater one) is the hero's insufficiently motived delay. He resolves to kill the murderer in the first act; but, as in the case of Hieronimo, the revenging father of the *Spanish Tragedy*, he fails to kill him, with not the best of reasons for his failure, until the end of the fifth. Throughout the play, indeed, the lead in the intrigue is taken not by the revenger but by the King. Claudius thrusts; Hamlet, in the main, but parries.

The delay was a weakness of the story even in Belleforest, but in Kyd it was made a more conspicuous one. In Belleforest there is no ghost, no disclosure, no mandate to revenge, no eager filial vow. Hamlet grows up with the spirit of revenge rankling in him; but he simply bides his time, stepping clear of the traps set in his path. There is no apparent reason for his delay—though for ten long years it continues—but there is also no reason for immediate revenge. Kyd, with his swift dramatic beginning, changed the situation, put a revenger already resolved into a waiting rôle, and, though he must have made the attempt, could not, from all appearances, have succeeded in plausibly adjusting the one to the other.

Both of the improbabilities mentioned were first noticed by the author[12] of *Some Remarks on the Tragedy of Hamlet, Prince of Denmark*, a pamphlet of 1736; and the explanation which he offers is that "had Hamlet gone naturally and promptly to work there would have been an end of our play."[13] Though this is obvious, it sounds shallow and frivolous; but it

---

direction puts it) they "play" before the King, Queen, and Court, an apparently harmless diversion turns abruptly into a tragic mêlée, involving performers and spectators in a common doom. Professor Creizenach seems to me to decline to face the facts. If Kyd could have contrived the dénouement of the *Spanish Tragedy*, he could certainly have contrived, in its essentials, that of *Hamlet*; and a tragic ending of some sort he had to contrive, for by the Senecan tragic strut and trappings he had adopted in the play he was committed to it.

[11] In this paragraph and at other points in the article, I am indebted to Professor Lewis's *Genesis of Hamlet*. Much of my indebtedness to him and to others, however, is difficult to indicate, so intricately interwoven are the borrowed ideas with ideas that they would not care to have attributed to them.

[12] Commonly said to be Sir Thomas Hanmer, the editor of the Oxford edition; but it has, with good reason, been denied.

[13] P. 33.

is not so shallow and frivolous as it sounds. Surely we need no longer cling to the fiction that a play is more than a play, or that Shakespeare is any more above somewhat arbitrarily deferring his conclusion than, in the *Œdipus Tyrannus*, was Sophocles. Of this and how many other fine dramas (and novels) it is to be said that had the hero or heroine gone promptly or most naturally to work—*plus de pièce possible!* In the case before us, from the point of view of psychology—but that, I think, was not his point of view[14]—Shakespeare had attempted an almost impossible task; from the point of view of mere dramaturgy—and this I think was his point of view—he had attempted a sufficiently difficult one. He was rewriting; but even if he were free to pick and choose he could hardly do it. The beginning and the end as they stood in Kyd offered dangerous but irresistible attractions. The end must stand as it was in Kyd because, in Shakespeare's hands, it was to make a brilliant stage catastrophe; and, at the same time, by presenting the fulfilment of the revenge, give an effect of unity and emphasis such as is to be found in all the great revenge tragedies in literature,—those of Æschylus, Sophocles, Euripides, and Alfieri. The beginning must stand as it was in Kyd because, in Shakespeare's hands, it was to make a marvel of exposition, possibly the greatest first act in all the range of drama; and, at the same time, by presenting the disclosure of the crime and the delivery of the mandate, give an effect of unity and completeness such as is to be found in the best Elizabethan plays. Just there was the rub, indeed. The Greeks were interested only in the end of the story on the stage; the Elizabethans, also, in the beginning. Kyd had united the Elizabethan and the classical technique in a revenge play, where they are incompatible. For even in the classical revenge plays there is long delay involved. As it defers her own dearest desire Electra repeatedly complains of it in the tragedy of Sophocles.[15] Years elapse in the old epical legends (here reduced within the limits of drama) as they do in the old story of Saxo and Belleforest.[16] But in the Greek drama they do not elapse on the stage—only the last day or so of the period is there presented. The ancients, in consequence, had really only the fifth act to fit and furnish out. Kyd had four acts, once the action was started; but the worst of it was that the intrigue that he put into them was not the revenger's but the murderer's, as he took it from

---

[14] As this is a point on which I have, in other connections, frequently insisted, I do not dwell on it here. See especially my *Othello* (1915).

[15] "He is ever yearning to be with us, but, though he yearns, he never resolves" (l. 170).—"He promises to come; but he never fulfils the promise" (318-20).—"Thou didst oft send me secret messages, thy heralds, saying that thou thyself wouldst appear as an avenger" (1155).—These complaints are really equivalent to Hamlet's self-reproaches, or the murmurings of his kinswomen against Hieronimo (*v. infra*, p. 15 ff.), but they are not meant to suggest a serious defect in the hero.

[16] Ten years, here; but in the Orestes story the child has to grow to manhood.

his source.[17]   The setting of his "mousetrap" of a play and the drawing of his sword on the King at prayer are the only instances of Hamlet's taking the offensive.   A revenger, who for four acts has little or nothing to do, must be a dubious and sorry figure; and yet this revenger was certainly meant for an heroic one.[18]   How, then, could Shakespeare as he took up the story, save his hero?   He could not, without inventing for his four acts a new intrigue, whereby the King should not so much catch Hamlet as Hamlet catch the King.[19]   For that sort of intrigue, as we shall see, he had little taste.   Moreover, he was, in general, "economical of invention"; and, for that matter, a new intrigue would make a different story!   How could Shakespeare save his hero, then, and also keep his plot?   Critics generally have thought that he did not save him, but grounded the delay in Hamlet's weakness and irresolution.   Still, the author of *Some Remarks* took him for a hero in his day—"so brave and careless of his own life,"—and everybody we know of from Shakespeare's day up to near the end of the eighteenth century did the same.   And I shall try to show that in doing so they were right; and that Shakespeare saved him, or endeavored to save him, in part as Kyd had contrived to save his hero before him, in part by having recourse, not to psychology, but to hedging and finesse.

2

First, as for the fact that he did save him—for Shakespeare's own time, if not for our time—and that Hamlet then and for long after was a hero, not merely the leading character.   The play, of course, is one of the great English institutions.   There is abundant evidence that no other play has been seen or read by so many people in the three centuries since its birth.   That of itself is evidence for the heroic quality of the leading character, at least in so far as he touches the popular imagination.   By morbid, realistic figures, weak or vacillating characters, the popular imagination cannot be touched.   The imagination of the people—and of the English people

---

[17] In Belleforest, Hamlet, until his return from England, does nothing—save sharpen his stakes—toward the fulfilment of the revenge.   Kyd added the experiment on the conscience of the King, the play-within-the-play.

[18] That is, like Hieronimo.   On this head scholars seem agreed.

[19] One other thing the dramatist might have done—put Hamlet in a quandary, and let him deliberate and debate through an act or two, like a hero of Corneille's or Schiller's Wallenstein, before coming to a decision.   But for that he had no technique.   Always his heroes make up their minds on the instant, or, like Othello, Brutus, and Macbeth, in a scene; and Hamlet makes up his as soon as ever the Ghost has spoken.   And having once made it up, he never changes it, but only reproaches himself for not acting to suit.   For reasoning, argument, the weighing of issues dramatically in the balance after the style of the French, Shakespeare had no models, but perhaps required none.   It was not the approaches to a decision that interested him, but the decision, the passions which arise out of it, the deed, and preceding and ensuing deeds.   And, this being so, when the deed is perforce postponed, these reproaches, which in an external way explain or motivate it, need not be interpreted as indicating native irresolution any more than, on the other hand, do the dramatic debates of the French.   See below, p. 50.

in particular—is simple and healthy, is romantic.[20]   English popular drama is romantic, above all the Elizabethan.   Shakespeare is romantic, through and through.   Indeed, it is in terms of pure romance that Lord Bacon, who did so much to lay bare what was real in the natural world about him, defines, in the very years when Hamlet was rewritten, the nature of poetry:

> The use of this feigned history hath been to give some shadow of satisfaction to the mind of man in those points wherein the nature of things doth deny it, the world being in proportion inferior to the soul; by reason whereof, there is, agreeable to the spirit of man, a more ample greatness, a more exact goodness, and a more absolute variety, than can be found in the nature of things.   Therefore, because the acts or events of true history have not that magnitude which satisfieth the mind of man, poesy feigneth acts and events greater and more heroical.—*Adv. Learning*, II, iv, 2.

And it is such that poesy feigns in Elizabethan tragedy, when it comes fully into its own.   "A more exact goodness," while it is still in the leading-strings of Seneca, it may not always present, but at least it presents "a more ample greatness," and "acts and events greater and more heroical."   And at all times, Shakespeare, like nearly all the other Elizabethans, presents, in tragedy, not men but supermen, either heroes or villain-heroes.   The fact is that it was only when Hamlet was played as a romantic hero, as he was, both in England and in Germany, in the seventeenth and eighteenth centuries, that he firmly held the stage.   As he became something of a morbid, pathological figure the play became something of a "highbrow," or closet, play.   And in so far as he holds the stage still it is largely because he is played more romantically than literary people conceive him.

From the beginning *Hamlet* has been continually referred to in print. And surely it is a remarkable thing that among the scores of references to the play (whether it be Kyd's or Shakespeare's) in sixteenth and seventeenth century literature, there is no suggestion of any shortcoming in him whatever.[21]   Such is the case even in the eighteenth century, when the comments on the Shakespearean characters grow numerous and extensive, and philosophers like Shaftesbury or dramatists like Fielding have more than a word to say of him, and whole essays are penned like *Some Remarks on the Tragedy of Hamlet* (63 pages), in 1736, and the *Miscellaneous Observations on the Tragedy of Hamlet*, in 1752.   Not till 1780 and 1784, when England is falling under the spell of Romanticism, does there arise a sentimentalist like Henry Mackenzie,[22] author of the *Man of Feeling*, or a University professor like William Richardson (both writers

---

[20] Even when the national literature is distinguished for realism, as is the Spanish, the popular drama is romantic.   Lope de Vega and Calderon are even farther removed from realism than Shakespeare.— As for the meaning, in this connection, of the word "romanticism," see below, p. 12, note 33

[21] See the Shakespeare Allusion-Book, and Mr. Munro's supplement (which appeared shortly before his untimely death at Gallipoli) in *Modern Philology*.

[22] *The Mirror*, No. 99, April 18, 1780.   He anticipates much of Goethe's criticism, even some of the phrases.   Richardson first wrote in 1774, but then he found Hamlet to be without fault.

and readers, we remember, not dramatists or theatre-goers) to say, Here, and here, thou ailest, and lay his finger on the spot. In earlier times, moreover, when Shakespeare's Hamlet first came on the boards, no one took note of any difference in the hero, thus born again, or remarked that this one, morally, was of weaker stuff. This last, to be sure, is only negative evidence, and, since most of the allusions in the seventeenth century are brief and cursory, not of moment; but as for the other evidence, Falstaff is continually alluded to in the period as cowardly and boastful, and Othello as jealous, and yet Hamlet—Kyd's or Shakespeare's either—who is mentioned oftener than any character save Falstaff himself, is never once called weak, vacillating, self-deceptive, melancholy, or anything else[23] that indicates a moral or mental defect, down to Mackenzie's and Richardson's day. This unanimity of opinion in Hamlet's favor, from the earliest times to within a little more than a century, is signal and striking. "Every reader and every audience," says Richardson himself before he marshals his arguments, "have hitherto taken part with Hamlet. They have not only pitied but esteemed him; and the voice of the people, in poetry as well as in politics, deserves some attention."[24] To be sure it does—was it not for the people that the play was penned?

3

There is no Allusion-Book, unfortunately, for the eighteenth century, and much of importance must have escaped me. But among those who say more than a word or a sentence about Hamlet as a character, and manifest an interest in him, are such authors as Rowe, Dennis, the Earl of Shaftesbury, Aaron Hill, Fielding, Warburton, Johnson, Voltaire, the Abbé Prévost, William Guthrie, the historian, who wrote the *Essay on English Tragedy*, Mrs. Griffith, who wrote the *Morality of Shakespeare's Dramas*, Frederick Pilon, the actor and dramatist, Tom Davies, the actor and the biographer of Garrick, and Edmund Malone. Many of these are not famous names; but some of those which are not famous, such as Guthrie and Pilon, are borne by sensible, enlightened, and fairly skilful writers. For evidence, it is perhaps the better that they are not all above the level of the throng: they come nearer to representing the public for which this stage play was written.

And what have they to say? Nicholas Rowe, in 1709, has, in his "Account of the Life" prefixed to his edition of the poet, a great deal to say of Hamlet but nothing of Hamlet's tragic fault. John Dennis, in 1712, complains that poetic justice is lacking.[25] James Drake had, in 1699, shown at length in the case of the other characters that "Nothing in

---

[23] Except that, in the earlier eighteenth century, he is called ferocious. (See below, p. 57.)

[24] *Additional Observations on Hamlet* (1784), p. 150.

[25] Essay on the *Genius and Writings of Shakespeare*, p. 9.

Antiquity can rival this Plot for the admirable distribution of Poetick Justice."[26]   The only cause that Dennis now can discover for the Prince's perishing with the guilty is his "design to kill his Uncle," and that he rightly holds "justify'd by no less than a Call from Heaven."   And though endowed with finer insight and taste, the author of *Some Remarks* is similarly troubled.   But he bethinks himself that "if Hamlet's virtue is not rewarded as we could wish, Mr. Addison's Maxim should satisfy us, which is this, 'That no man is so thoroughly Virtuous as to claim a Reward in Tragedy, or to have Reason to repine at the Dispensations of Providence.' "[27]   Aaron Hill, in 1735, and the Abbé Prévost, in 1738, give, the one, two pages, and the other, four, to an account of the play and the hero, but find no tragic fault and notice no procrastination.[28]   The same may be said of Fielding, the novelist and dramatist, who frequently refers to Hamlet, and in *Tom Jones* describes Garrick's acting at length. William Guthrie, in 1760 (1747? 1749?), as he praises Shakespeare's heroes for the variety and simple truth of their humanity, without tragic trappings, remarks:

> All that we see in Hamlet is a well-meaning, sensible young man, but full of doubts and perplexities even after the resolution is fixed.   In this character there is nothing but what is common to the rest of mankind; he has no marking, no colouring, but its beautiful drawing, perhaps, cost Shakespeare more than any other figure he ever attempted.[29]

Voltaire discusses Hamlet on several occasions, but nowhere betrays a suspicion of a weakness in his character; and in his *Plan de la Tragédie d'Hamlet*, in 1761, clearly shows that he takes it that Hamlet spares the King at prayer for the reason given, and thinks it is the King that he stabs when it is Polonius.   Johnson, in his edition of 1765, is evidently troubled by Hamlet's delay in executing the revenge, and calls him "an instrument rather than an agent."   "After he has, by the stratagem of the play, convicted the King, he makes no attempt to punish him; and his death is at last effected by an incident which Hamlet had no part in producing." But Johnson is finding fault, not with the hero, but with the play.   "The gallant Hamlet" the moralizing Mrs. Griffith calls him in 1775;[30] and if she points no moral on the evils of procrastination, we may depend upon it that it is only because she finds none.   Frederick Pilon, in 1777, in his essay of twenty-five pages, *On the Character of Hamlet as performed by Mr. Henderson at the Theatre Royal*, discusses not only Henderson but Hamlet at

---

[26] *Allusion-Book*, ii, pp. 424-25.   See below, p. 64.

[27] P. 60.

[28] *Tome* xiv, pp. 68-72.   The Abbé, the reader may be reminded, admired Shakespeare and read him in English.   (Jusserand, *Shakespeare in France*.)   For Hill see the *Prompter*, October 24, 1735.   (Copy at Yale.)

[29] *Op. cit.*, p. 21.

[30] P. 516.

length, finds no flaw in his metal, and treats not only the sparing of the King at prayer but also the assumption of madness and the device of the Mousetrap in a way that excludes the possiblity of any evasion on his part or of self-deception. Tom Davies, in 1784, gives a hundred and fifty pages in his *Dramatic Miscellanies* to a discussion of *Hamlet* in its relation to the stage; but he seems not to have heard of Mackenzie's or Richardson's opinions, and finds fault only with the hero's ferocity, whether in his "horrid soliloquy" as he spares the King, or in his treatment of Rosencrantz and Guildenstern. "Hamlet is not a character for imitation; there are many features of it that are disagreeable";[31] but vacillation, it appears, is not to be numbered among them. And Edmund Malone, having in 1790, reproduced in a couple of pages of fine print the most important passages of criticism in *Some Remarks* (of 1736), where Hamlet appears as an estimable and heroic figure, adds his express approval.

4

Before Mackenzie's day, then, there was, so far as we can discover from popular and literary opinion concerning Hamlet, nothing wrong with him. He was a gallant, romantic figure, instrument and (at last) victim of fate. The most remarkable thing, perhaps, to be noted in our survey is the fact that at the close of the seventeenth century and the beginning of the eighteenth, when the moralizing and classicizing tendency was at its zenith, critics and censors such as Jeremy Collier, James Drake, and John Dennis, who could hardly, of course, have been expected to discover in him anything psychological, did not even find poetic justice fulfilled on the head of the hesitating prince. Shaftesbury himself, in 1711, says of "that piece of his [Shakespeare's] which appears to have most affected English hearts, and has perhaps been oftenest acted of any which have come upon our stage," that it "is almost one continued moral." But by that he means only "a series of deep reflections drawn from one mouth, upon the subject of one single accident and calamity,"[32] not a moral to be derived from the chief character's conduct. And Drake, though he declares that the "Moral of it [the play] is excellent," and traces the "distribution of Poetick Justice" in detail and with delight, showing how "they [the wicked] are taken in their own Toyls,"—Polonius, Guildenstern and Rosencrantz, Laertes and the King,—has for Hamlet's own conduct or misconduct never a word. Dramatists so imbued and saturated with classical theory as Nicholas Rowe, Aaron Hill, and Samuel Johnson would have discovered in Hamlet a tragic fault, you would think, or

---

[31] Ed. 1784, iii, 143. I might add to the list Charles Jennens, who also, in the twelve pages of his "sketch of the play," prefixed to his edition of 1773, nowhere betrays a suspicion of weakness, self-deception, or any other fault or defect; and Richardson himself (*v. supra* n. 22) in 1774.

[32] *Characteristics*, ed. Robertson (N. Y. 1900), *i*, p. 180.

would have had none of him. Actually they find in him nothing either
psychologically or morally faulty, but hold him to be an heroic nature,
instrument and victim of fate together.

The psychological, the morbid Hamlet, the realistic Hamlet, so to speak,
is, we must conclude, exclusively the discovery, or invention, of the Romantic Age.[33] At this Professor Bradley rejoices, and finds it particularly significant that he came to light only "when the slowly rising sun of Romance
began to flush the sky."[34] The deeper, subtler spirit abroad, that is to
say, detected him. If it were a delicate and elusive matter that was in
question, this might well be. But I cannot be so sure of the reality of a
tragic fault in the hero of a great popular tragedy (the centre and pivot
of the tragedy, indeed) not discovered in the two centuries nearest to it, not
discovered by a moral philosopher like Shaftesbury, by dramatists like Rowe,
Fielding, and Hill, or by the massive mind of Samuel Johnson (moralist
and dramatist, too) which sought for it and was troubled for the lack of it,
and first brought to light by Scotch professors and sentimentalists, and
the rest of the Romanticists who knew not and loved not the stage or its
ways. We go a bit deeper than the seventeenth and eighteenth centuries,
no one will deny; but the seventeenth and eighteenth centuries are far
nearer in time and spirit to Shakespeare and the people for whom he played
and wrote. Nor is time the only factor. The present Hamlet theory
arose and was developed far away from every tradition and echo of the
stage. It arose in a land where the theatre was anathema; it was developed, in the hands of Coleridge, by a dreamer, philosopher, and maker of
closet-plays; it was perfected in Germany, Coleridge's foster-land—then,
at least, a land of dreamers, philosophers, and makers of closet-plays. So too
arose the prevailing interpretations of Shylock, Falstaff, and Othello, which I
have questioned and impugned elsewhere. They are not therefore to be
rejected, to be sure,—because they are in origin literary and Romantic,
German or Scotch. But when such interpretations of early drama can be
shown to have broken sharply with tradition they should be scrutinized
with care. It is the poetry of the Romantic epoch that is of enduring value,
—not its criticism but the poetry of its criticism. And in its criticism
of early literature—epic, ballad, and drama alike—poetry overwhelmed
history, the spirit of the present the spirit of the past. Indeed it was of
the essence of Romantic criticism to break with tradition or ignore it.

[33] It is unnecessary to remind the reader of the poverty of the language, and of the fact that the idea
involved in the word *romantic*, as used on pp. 7-8 above, has little in common with that involved in the
word here. No word is more difficult of definition; but a measure of the difference between the meaning
of it as applied to Elizabethan art and to the art of the close of the eighteenth century is supplied by this
very change wrought in the interpretation of Hamlet. For, like every age, the Romantic had a Hamlet
after its own heart and in its own image. If the Romantic Hamlet, as compared to the true Elizabethan,
is realistic, it is only as Werther is morbid and realistic.

[34] *Shakespearean Tragedy* (1908), p. 92.

The Romanticists believed, above all, in genius, genius omnipotent as a god, self-taught and self-impelled. They did not conceive of genius as utterly dependent, potent only as it absorbed all the living thoughts and sentiments of the period and was initiated into the newest mysteries of the craft. It is only so that even a lyric poet can reach and move his audience, and how much more the writer for the public stage! And if it is only so—through the medium of tradition and convention—that this greatest of dramatists reached and moved his audience, how otherwise than as we become acquainted with that tradition and convention shall we ourselves, in a later age, come in contact with him?

CHAPTER II

HAMLET'S FAULT IN THE LIGHT OF OTHER TRAGEDIES

If such be the opinion of Hamlet in the seventeenth and eighteenth centuries, what way is there left to judge between them and us but to appeal to Shakespeare himself, and, as best we may, inquire what he intended. To the business of this inquiry we now turn.

1

The only fault, as we have seen, that the eighteenth century discovered, was, in so far as the two can be separated, in the play and not in the man. "The Poet . . was obliged to delay his Hero's Revenge," observes the author of *Some Remarks;* "but then he should have contrived some good Reason for it."[1] Though for this critic it was a matter of deficient motivation, he did not look for the motive in psychology. Yet to us, in our modern preoccupation with character, it would seem as if Shakespeare had deliberately manipulated his fable so as to place the motive there. Kyd himself had attempted to justify the delay. And he did this, if we are to take the evidence of the *Fratricide Punished* and the *Spanish Tragedy,* by three means: by introducing guards about the King to make access difficult; by turning the feigned madness to account to make access easier; and by giving an appropriate character to the hero. Of the three, Shakespeare employs only the last—characterization. In doing so the only motives presented for the delay are: the hero's aversion to the deed, but once directly expressed ("Oh cursed spite," etc.); his doubt of the Ghost; his desire to kill the King when engaged in some act of wickedness instead of when at prayer; and the cowardice and neglect of duty of which he vaguely and contradictorily accuses himself.

The external motivation which Shakespeare omitted we discuss below. As for that in the character, most of it no doubt had in some form been already used by Kyd. His doubt of the Ghost is like Hieronimo's doubt of Belimperia's message inciting him to revenge;[2] and, besides, it seems needed as an occasion for the play-within-the-play. This, too, must have been in the old *Hamlet,* because the same striking device is employed in the *Spanish Tragedy* as well as in the *Fratricide Punished.* Kyd's, again, must have been the sparing for fearful ulterior purposes of the King at prayer; for it is far more like him than like Shakespeare,[3] and it not only is in the *Fratricide Punished* but also seems to be imitated in Marston's *Antonio's*

---

[1] P. 33.

[2] *Spanish Tragedy*, III, ii, 34 ff.

[3] See below, p. 53.

Revenge[4] (1599-1600), a play, like all of this dramatist's early ones, deeply affected by Kyd's influence. And the charges of remissness and neglect of duty brought against Hamlet (our present concern) are quite similar to those brought against Hieronimo. However all these devices may have been further developed by Shakespeare, they are, then, nothing new; and as used by others before him, they were not meant, as we shall see, to indicate a weakness in the hero's character.

2

Hieronimo, indeed, who in dramatic function (save that he is a father instead of a son) is almost a replica of Hamlet, made a similar impression upon contemporary writers. He is alluded to in sixteenth and seventeenth century literature almost as frequently; though, as in Hamlet's case, madness is the characteristic of his generally remarked upon. No other infirmity is discovered. But he reproaches himself almost as bitterly as the Danish Prince,—

> See, see, oh see thy shame, Hieronimo,—

and he also incurs the reproaches of others. Hamlet is rebuked only by the Ghost. Here the equivalent to the Ghost in the bedchamber is only Hieronimo's crazy fancy as he looks Senex in the face; but this appears to the same dramatic purpose:

> And art thou come, Horatio from the deapth,
> To ask for justice in this upper earth,
> To tell thy father thou art unreveng'd?
> *Baz.* Ah, my good Lord, I am not your young sonne.
> *Hier.* What, not my sonne? thou then a furie art,
> Sent from the emptie Kingdome of black night
>
> . . . .
>
> To plague Hieronimo that is remisse,
> And seekes not vengeance for Horatioes death.
> > III, xiii, 132.

Besides, there is Belimperia, sweetheart of his murdered son, who apostrophizes him from out of her window:

> Hieronimo, why writ I of thy wrongs?
> Or why art thou so slacke in thy revenge?
> > III, ix, 7.

And, face to face, she reproaches him thus:

[4] In Act III, i, 136-40, where Antonio offers to stab Piero, but says,

> No, not so.
> This shall be sought for; I'll force him feed on life
> Till he shall loath it. This shall be the close
> Of Vengeance' strain.

In the last line and a half Marston gives away the revenge-plot formula. Mr. J. D. Wilson, in the article in the *Library*, cited above p. 2, note 3, finds Hamlet's speech in the prayer-scene, like his soliloquy "To be or not to be," mainly "pre-Shakespearean." (p. 179.)

> Is this the loue thou bearst Horatio?
> Is this the kindness that thou counterfeits?
> Are these the fruits of thine incessant teares?
> Hieronimo, are these thy passions,
> Thy protestations, and thy deep lamentes,
> That thou were wont to wearie men withall?
> O unkind father, O deceitfull world,
> With what excuses canst thou show thyselfe,
> With what dishonour and the hate of men
> From this dishonour and the hate of men?[5]
>
> IV, i, 1-10.

And there is Isabella, who reproaches Hieronimo before she kills herself:

> Make haste, Hieronimo, to holde excusde
> Thy negligence in pursute of their deaths
> Whose hatefull wrath bereu'd him of his breath.
> Ah nay, thou doest delay their deaths,
> Forgiues the murderers of thy noble sonne.
>
> IV, ii, 29.

Thus, though Hieronimo's reproaches against himself are less vigorous than Hamlet's, they are so far reinforced by the reproaches of his relatives that he seems to carry even a heavier burden of blame.   Madness, it would seem, would alone exonerate him; but he is not mad consistently and continuously; and save for the reproaches, he is presented, anyone would admit, as a character without blemish.   Rightly viewed, his reproaches, like his kinswomen's, seem to take the form only of murmurings and complaints, as if he—as if they too—well knew that he could do the deed and that in time he would.

The old Hamlet, in all likelihood, was presented in much the same way. He may even have been reproached by others,—by Horatio, as well as by the Ghost on his second visit.   However that be, it now seems probable that a reproach may, in effect, be no more than an exhortation; and of this sort in the main are the Ghost's and Hamlet's own:

> Do you not come your tardy son to chide
> That, lapst in time and passion, lets go by
> The important acting of your dread command?
>
> *Ghost.*   Do not forget, this visitation
> Is but to whet thy almost blunted purpose.

That may be, not a judgment on Hamlet's character, but a reflection on his conduct in this particular matter, with a practical end in view.   The Ghost at least is not nearly so hard on the young Prince as are Belimperia and Isabella on Hieronimo.   In any case, the Ghost and Hamlet too take it for granted that the youth is equal to the task.   The Ghost reproaches

---

[5] *Sic,* in the suspicious text.

Hamlet; Hamlet chides himself: but no doubt of his powers or intentions is ever expressed by either.

So it is in Seneca. Mere exhortation, not damaging revelation of character, is the function of self-reproaches in the old Latin dramatist, artistic sponsor of Kyd and Marston, and creator of the revenge-play type. In the *Thyestes* Atreus broods over his remissness somewhat like Hieronimo and Hamlet.

> O Soul so sluggish, spiritless, and weak,[6]

he cries; but like them, it would seem, he is not ordinarily sluggish and not spiritless or weak at all. And the same, of course, may be said of those far from weak or spiritless ladies, Medea and Clytemnestra, who chide and scold themselves only to spur themselves on.

> Why, sluggish soul, dost thou safe counsel seek?
> Why hesitate?[7]

cries the latter. In these cases, to be sure, there is no such long interval of delay as in *Hamlet;* but delay of some sort there is in all classical and Renaissance revenge tragedies, and these exhortations serve to motive it. They motive it, that is, not in the psychological sense of grounding it in character, but of explaining it and bridging it over. They motive it by reminding the audience that the main business in hand, though retarded, is not lost to view. They motive it by showing the audience that the hero, even in his delay, is a conscious and responsible and (so far) consistent being. In short, they give a reason for the delay, not the "good" and fundamental reason demanded by the author of *Some Remarks*, but a better reason than none. They provide an epical motive, if I may so call it, rather than a dramatic one.

3

How much the dramatist was bent on motiving the story without impairing the prestige of the hero appears from the nature of the reproach. "Forgetting" and "tardiness" are the burden of it. "Remember me," cries the Ghost at parting. "Do not forget," he adjures his son when he reappears to him in the Queen's bedchamber. "Tardy," "bestial oblivion," "letting all sleep,"—such are the charges that Hamlet brings against

---

[6] "Ignave, iners, enervis," etc. l. 176. Cf. also the following:

> Quid stupes? tandem incipe
> Animosque sume.   *Thyestes*, 241-42.
> Anime, quid rursus times
> Et ante rem subsidis?   Audendum est, age. *Ib.* 283-5.
> Male agis, recedis, anime: si parces tuis,
> Parces et illis.   *Ib.* 324-25.

[7] Quid, segnis anime, tuta consilia expetis?
Quid fluctuaris? *Ag.* ll. 108-9.

himself.   He suffers capability and godlike reason to fust in him unused.[8]
So it is with Hieronimo:—he calls himself "remisse"; Belimperia calls
him "slacke"; and Isabella bewails his "negligence."[9] How much more
it is a matter of story than of character, particularly this forgetting!
Psychologically taken, how could Hamlet forget—"while memory holds
a seat in this distracted globe"!—and remember anything else? But he
remembers everything else, and is not oblivious, neglectful, or tardy, for all
that you would expect him to be, in any other matter.   As a motive or
link in a story, however, the device, though a makeshift, is not uncommon.
How, in real life, could Edgar, Albany, and the rest forget King Lear until
Kent enters to remind them, or forget Cordelia until she is hanged? "Great
thing of us forgot," cries Edgar;—and yet this thing was all that he cared
for, and what was happening to Edmund and the demon sisters was nothing
to him at all.   But plot, tragic effect demanded that Cordelia should die,
and that the entrance of Lear with her body should come only after the
minor matters had been disposed of.   Hence the dramatic and climactic
postponement, the forgetting which explains it but (for us) needs itself to be
explained.   A closer parallel is in a play of Lope de Vega's.   In Act III
of *El Marqués de las Navas* (1624) the Ghost of Leonardo appears to
the Marquis, who had killed him in a rash quarrel, to seek protection
for his betrothed. (As in *Hamlet*, the Ghost appears to others besides
the person whom he seeks, withdraws with him to tell his tale in a
secluded spot, and just before he leaves bids him "not forget" (*no os
descuidéis*)) Later in the same act, the next night presumably, he
appears again, and complains to the Marquis of his "forgetfulness" and
"neglect."   Yet forgetfulness or neglect does not seem in any other way
to be the Marquis' characteristic.   And there is the still less plausible
lapse of memory which Voltaire finds it necessary to ascribe to Œdipus
in order to explain why he had not suspected himself of the murder of
Laius long before.[10]   And as for dilatoriness, there is the parallel in the
Adelphi of Terence.   "Why didn't I   tell my father all about it?"

---

[8] These expressions quite contradict the Coleridgean theory, as do the facts in the story. But to
those who can treat the text as a document rather than as a play this circumstance presents no difficulty.
"So sehr steht er unter dem Bann seiner Reflexion, dass er zu Zeiten glauben kann, er denke noch zu wenig
—eine Erwägung die mich immer aufs Tiefste erschüttert" (Bulthaupt, ii, p. 248).   That is, a soliloquy
need not necessarily serve for the spectator's enlightenment, and a dramatist may as well put him on
the wrong track as on the right.

[9] See above, pp. 15-16; also, *Spanish Tragedy*, III, xiii, 106, 156.

[10] *Œdipe*, IV, i:

> Enfin je me souviens qu'aux champs de la Phocide
> (Et je ne conçois pas par quel enchantement
> J'oubliais jusq'ici ce grand événement;
> La main des dieux sur moi si longtemps suspendue
> Semble ôter le bandeau qu'ils mettaient sur ma vue),
> Dans un chemin étroit je trouvai deux guerriers,
>   etc.

Æschinus asks himself after he has got into trouble . . . "I have been dilatory all this time."[11]   And his father, when he learns the truth, remarks, "You hesitated and hesitated, and ten months have passed away."[12]   As Æschinus himself admits, his father was just the man to be indulgent— such a father is needed by the dramatist at the end—but if Æschinus had told him, there would have been no end for the play, nor even a beginning.

In all these cases reproaches before the deed do not, it seems, discredit the hero.   Sins of omission, on the stage of the Renaissance, are not like sins of commission, if they be sins at all.   They did not discredit Hieronimo and Hamlet in their day, or Shakespeare's Hamlet, who, unlike the other, kept the stage, in the two centuries after.   It is only as, in later times, men forsook the playhouse and took up their spectacles and the text, that they mistook the simple intention of its technique, and began to turn the words which motive the retardation of the story into an analysis of character.   And indeed the older technique, though rightly it seems to us naïve, is in this case truer to life than ours.   Hieronimo, Marston's Antonio, and Hamlet are meant to be fine and noble souls, and why should they not hesitate and delay?   Not in every man who does that is there a vital defect.   "Yea, a man will pause," replies the Chorus to the complaint of Sophocles' Electra, "on the verge of a great work."   Who, in real life, does not?   Or as Sir Arthur Quiller-Couch has put it, "Men in this world do not post off to stab other men on the affidavit of a ghost . . . why should such a man as Hamlet not shrink from the deed and cast about for new incentives?"   And why should he not then reproach himself for shrinking?

There is a defect in the drama, of course, but it is only as our technique is superimposed upon the drama that this is turned into a tragic defect in the hero, or that by his straightforward and magnanimous complaints and reproaches he is made to take the stand against himself.   How far we go in this putting upon the older drama of the form and fashion of our own appears from the treatment recently given to the Orestes of the *Choephori*. Professor Wilamowitz-Moellendorff[13] finds traces of hesitation and unwillingness to do the deed in the long preliminary lamentations of the princely youth for his father and in the appeals to him and the gods.   The reason is (though he does not say so) that otherwise they are for the critic not dramatic enough—being the mere utterance of emotion, simple lamentation, invocation, or prayer.   To him, as to the Hamlet critics, the interval between the resolve and the deed must mean something—something inward and psychological.   For the Greek it only made the deed more momentous. Such is the difference between the ancient (or Elizabethan) and the modern,

[11] L. 630.
[12] L. 690.
[13] In his translation of the *Choephori*, introduction, pp. 147-49.

between a Greek and a German. But it is a difference which it is the
function of scholarship to mediate, a gulf which scholarship alone can bridge.

4

In the soliloquies, to be sure, Hamlet also roundly abuses himself. In
the soliloquy at the end of the second act—"O what a rogue and peasant
slave am I"—he contrasts his own sluggishness with the Player's passion,
and dubs himself a rogue, a dull and muddy-mettled rascal, a peaking
John-a-dreams, an ass, a coward. "Am I a coward?" he cries, catching
himself, or his manhood rebounding, as it were, against the charge:

> Who calls me villain, breaks my pate across,
> Plucks off my beard and blows it in my face,
> Tweaks me by the nose, gives me the lie i' the throat
> As deep as to the lungs, who does me this?

Echo answers, Who? and he rouses himself, and shakes off the slanders
he has been showering upon himself, like the true and sensible man that
he is. In another soliloquy, his last, he complains of himself again as he
enviously admires the energy and valor of Fortinbras:

> Now, whether it be
> Bestial oblivion, or some craven scruple
> Of thinking too precisely on the event,—
> A thought which, quarter'd, hath but one part wisdom
> And ever three parts coward,—I do not know
> Why yet I live to say, "This thing's to do,"
> Sith I have cause and will and strength and means
> To do't.

But here again the charge is unmade in the making. Here, though there
is more analysis, Hamlet himself accepts none of the alternatives that
offer. He "does not know"; he has "will and strength and means to do it";
—these are the last words, and it is they that stick in our minds. Shakespeare will not suffer him, after all, to testify against himself. What he
does is to let Hamlet pull himself together.[14]

[14] As it seems to me, this is the plain and natural interpretation, and for that reason, if for no other
to be accepted. Here is no pessimism, no despair, no doubt of himself. "What's wrong with me?" he
says, as any of us might do. "I haven't been myself of late." Certainly there is no mystery-mongering
on the part of the poet. The emphasis is not on "I do not know" but on the final clause; and there can
be no mystery if he has "strength and means and will to do it." Never before or after is a mystery hinted
at. To be sure, Hamlet does not know why he delays, either here or in his former soliloquy of self-reproach;
but that is because there is no reason why; and Shakespeare simply avails himself of the familiar fact
that now and then the most practical person in the world will say: "I don't know why I haven't done
that." Save for this, it would be strange indeed if Hamlet should not "know why," seeing that whenever
any other character of Shakespeare's concerns himself about his motives he knows them, even with a start-
ling exactness. The good know how good theirs are; the wicked, how wicked. And Hamlet is the
keenest-witted, the most introspective of the lot. All this, to be sure, runs counter to the common interpretation, that, unlike most characters, Hamlet is a real person, and that it is the authentic sign of his
reality that we cannot explain him—that he cannot explain himself. See Professor E. H. Wright's article
"Inconsistency in Characterization," in Columbia *Shakespearean Studies* (1916), especially pp. 390, 392.
Like many others, but unlike the poet, Mr. Wright makes much of the mystery here, identifying it
with the inscrutable mystery of the living soul;—but that I complain of him rather than of his predecessors
is due to the fact that he is nearest at hand, and is not only a scholar but, in this book, has the company
and countenance of scholars.

Several times I have had occasion, in my essays on Elizabethan subjects, to show that soliloquies are to pass current at their face value; and are the truth itself, not to be gainsaid, like the comment of prologue or chorus or of modern or ancient *raisonneur*. And this is no exception: that Hamlet should not give the audience a handle against himself the dramatist has taken good care.

Hamlet's words are not to be taken seriously, thinks Kuno Fischer,[15] because he reproaches himself. If it were in real life that would settle the matter; and of course it has some bearing here. In accusing himself he excuses himself, to turn the French phrase round. But Shakespeare's villains in soliloquy all lay bare their villainy, and cowards like Parolles do not stick at calling themselves cowards. That is a different thing, however; and that it is different is to the audience perfectly clear. Richard calls himself a villain, and Parolles a coward,[16] coolly, almost profession-ally, as if you were to say, "I am a butcher," or, "I am a cook." Neither reproaches or abuses himself. Hamlet calls himself coward, rogue, and rascal in a paroxysm of moral indignation. His words do not fit as Rich-ard's and Parolles' do. Why does he not speak of his malady—his mel-ancholy or weakness of will—if he has one, and sigh for sanity?[17] "Rogue," "rascal," and "coward" are evidently odds and ends of abuse that he snatches up and throws at himself, so to speak, to drive himself on. And the oc-casion for it is manifest: the example of the Player, first, and of the redoubt-able Fortinbras afterward. But there are no circumstances to make us discount the cool candor of Richard and Parolles. Richard owns up at his first appearance; Parolles, after we have already marked him as a coward for ourselves.[18] Whereas Hamlet's whole bearing and demeanor in the two acts previous to his first soliloquy of self-reproach nullify it. He is noble and intrepid there, and holds his life at a pin's fee. "Unhand me!" he cries when Horatio and the rest would hinder him from following the Ghost; "I'll make a ghost of him that lets me." And if now when we come upon this outburst of indignation and disgust we are for a moment tempted to mistake him, or think him faint-hearted at all, we remember him as we have seen and noted him before. Or if that should not satisfy us, we con-sider how he acquits himself presently,—in the bedchamber, on the voyage,

[15] *Hamlet* (1896), pp. 290-91.

[16] Richard, in his first soliloquy; Parolles, *A. W.*, IV, iii, 366.

[17] He speaks of "my weakness and my melancholy" only at the end of the soliloquy at the end of Act II, and then as of a possible means of the devil's deceiving him as to the Ghost. The melancholy were supposed especially subject to these visitations, or delusions. Cf. *White Devil*, III, iii, p. 79 (Hazlitt ed.); " 'Tis my melancholy." Cf. also below, p. 72, note 4.

[18] He is called such by Helena, in the first scene, both to his face and behind his back; and, in III, vi, by several persons whose words are presently to receive overt confirmation.

and at the fencing match.[19] Neither Parolles nor Richard, moreover, calls himself a rogue, a rascal, an ass. Save in a comedy, what ass ever did? In tragedy, in the life we lead which verges upon it, those who do that are sensible folk like you and me.

Most people, however, are not troubled by the convention of the veracious soliloquy; nor do they generally take Hamlet for a coward or rogue. They take him for a "moping John-a-dreams," instead. Of that charge Hamlet himself makes nothing; "coward" is the word that, after he flings it from him, he, in the end, grimly, sardonically, fits to his case.

> 'Swounds, I should take it, for it cannot be
> But I am pigeon-liver'd, and lack gall . . .

Or else people think that where there is so much smoke there must be some fire, and something is wrong with Hamlet that he dreams not of. But this matter of his self-deception we take up in the chapter below.

5

Confessions in soliloquy, moreover, are generally confirmed,—are, in Shakespeare's tragedy at least, never contradicted by the comment of other characters in a position to know, or by the confidences imparted to them by the character himself. Hamlet eventually tells Horatio of his uncle's guilt and his own purpose, but not of his difficulties or failures in carrying it out. To Horatio (or to himself, indeed) he never complains of any specific dereliction of duty such as sparing the King at prayer. Nor to any one is he known to have a defect. No one ever ventures to speak of him slightingly or critically. Why does not the King, Laertes, or Fortinbras despise him for a scholar and dreamer, at least, instead of taking him as they all do for the worthy son of his warrior sire? Why does not the Queen once sigh, or Horatio sadly shake his head? He is a courtier, soldier, scholar, the expectancy and rose of the fair state, cries Ophelia, and there is no suggestion that she is saying it as one who does not know. It is the accepted opinion. The King fears him, and shrinks from bringing him to account for Polonius' death, he says, because of the great love the general gender bear him. The sinful Queen quails under his rebuke, and yet loves him too well to betray his confidence. And, as often in Shakespeare's tragedies, at the end of the play judgment to the same effect is pronounced on his character by a disinterested party, like the chorus of the Greeks. The closing funeral orations, observes Professor Schick,

---

[19] See below, p. 28; also the eloquent passage in Professor Bradley's *Shakespearean Tragedy* (1908), p. 102, in which, though he finds Hamlet in a morbid state, he rightly contradicts the opinion that Hamlet is by nature anything of a weakling, whether before this or after. Though we take this point of view, it should, however, be remembered that both Mr. Bradley and I are far from taking the point of view of Werder and other German critics—that Hamlet was seeking not revenge but justice, and thus had attempted a task in itself impossible.

are always spoken by the dramatist himself.[20] "Let four captains," cries Fortinbras,

> Bear Hamlet, like a soldier, to the stage,
> For he was likely, had he been put on,
> To have proved most royally; and, for his passage,
> The soldiers' music and the rites of war
> Speak loudly for him.
> Take up the bodies. Such a sight as this
> Becomes the field, but here shows much amiss.
> Go, bid the soldiers shoot.

A royal salute is given. For no one else in death has Shakespeare let the trumpets blare and cannon thunder; but this youth,[21] says the man whom Hamlet himself had emulated, would have made a kingly king. It is like the judgment pronounced at the end by Cassio on Othello; like that pronounced by Antony on Brutus; and like that pronounced by Octavius on Antony himself and his queen. But in none of these cases is the praise so unmingled with blame, as if (were the poet to have his way) the villain, fate, and false fortune, not the hero himself, must bear the whole heavy burden. Critics there are who have thought that Fortinbras said it all in irony, but not those who are most in sympathy with Shakespeare's art.[22] So the words could not have been understood; or even if they had been, they would have disturbed that note of calm and reconciliation which Shakespeare in his great tragedies always reaches at the close. No respectable person in his dramas, for that matter, consciously or unconsciously speaks lightly of the dead. The poet's own personal humor, it would seem, did not sally across the confines of the frivolous or profane.

Here, or somewhere, one would have expected comment on Hamlet's shortcomings, his weakness or tragic fault. Instead, there is only praise from his friends, fear and hatred from his enemies. How is it possible, then, that a tragic fault or weakness could have been intended?[23a] Not only do Shakespeare's heroes know their faults, like Lear at the beginning, or Othello at the end, as Hamlet says he does not (and would seem to have none to know), but their friends and enemies know them too. The Fool and Kent know Lear's, Lady Macbeth her husband's, Enobarbus Antony's, Cassius Brutus', and Iago Othello's;[23b] but Horatio, Ophelia, Gertrude, Laertes, Fortinbras, who at the end avers that as a king he would have proved right royally, even Claudius himself, find in Hamlet no weakness at

[20] *I.e.*, so far as authority is concerned. Generally they are much in character, however, though in Octavius's eulogy of Antony it is hard to make this out.

[21] See below, p. 66, note 8.

[22] Cf. Professor Trench, *Shakespeare's Hamlet* (1913), pp. 238 ff. (The *Times* rightly demurred to such an opinion.)

[23a] Both Professor Baker and Professor Lewis have recently pointed out the fact that not always in Shakespeare is a tragic fault to be found.

[23b] And the pride of Coriolanus and the villainy of Richard are known to everybody.

all! Only Horatio, of course, who alone is in the secret of the murder, could know of the procrastination or suspect it. He does not even hint at it. But Laertes might at least have belittled his swordsmanship, Polonius his statesmanship, and Claudius at times might have questioned his formidableness as a foe.[24] Indeed, who so likely to know his own fault as Hamlet himself? At every other point (and at this as well!) he, like other Shakespearean characters, knows himself even as he is known.[25]

Nor can it be urged that Hamlet's defect is too private and delicate a matter to be touched upon. On the stage the secrets of the heart must rudely be brought to light; on the stage people know and talk about all sorts of things that no one would know or talk about off it. Even of our stage this is true, where there is greater reticence, and how much more is it true of the Elizabethan! Even Schiller and Ibsen must needs, in such cases, have recourse to comment, and they wrote for a more intellectual audience than Shakespeare's. Wallenstein too doubts, hesitates, procrastinates, though not, like Hamlet, episodically, but throughout the play. And he knows his own shortcoming, though at some points his friends know it better. Illo and the Countess know it: Terzky and Wrangel lay their fingers on or near the spot.[26] And Ibsen, who also wrote for audiences, not readers, though for audiences such as one seldom sees, found it necessary to bring Solness' apprehensions and Peer Gynt's indefinable evasions into the plain light of day. All the workmen know that the Masterbuilder cannot climb high towers, and openly his friends and enemies dissuade him from it or urge him on. And as for Peer Gynt, his career of hedging and dodging and "going round about" is made clear to us by

---

[24] See below, p. 28.

[25] A friend calls my attention to the fact that in thus interpreting Hamlet's reproaches, as well as in the general conception of Hamlet as not irresolute, I am following Swinburne, in his *Study of Shakespeare* (1895), pp. 161-69. I had not read this particular passage for some years:

"That Hamlet should seem at times to accept for himself, and even to enforce by reiteration of argument upon his conscience and his reason, some such conviction or suspicion as to his own character, tells much rather in disfavour than in favour of its truth. A man whose natural temptation was to swerve, whose inborn inclination was to shrink and skulk aside from duty and from action, would hardly be the first and last person to suspect his own weakness, the one only unbiassed judge and witness of sufficiently sharp-sighted candour and accuracy to estimate aright his poverty of nature and the malformation of his mind."

The only point at which I am constrained to dissent from the great poet's judgment is where, having recognized that "the signal characteristic of Hamlet's inmost nature is by no means irresolution or hesitation or any form of weakness," he adds, "but rather the strong conflux of contending forces." See above, p. 7, note 19. But he lets it go at that, and in the discussion as a whole he is as remarkable for his clearness of perception as his readers (*quorum pars!*) have been for their dulness. He wrote in 1879; how many have gone on writing since! But Swinburne foresaw how it would be; and after he shows how Shakespeare has endeavored to exhibit Hamlet's courage and resourcefulness in the expedition to England, he adds, with a still smile, the words quoted here on p. iv.

[26] *Illo:*   Der Einzige, der dir schadet, ist der Zweifel. (*Picc.*, II, vi.)
              Die Wahl ist's was ihm schwer wird; drängt die Noth,
              Dann kommt ihm seine Stärke. (*Picc.*, III, i.)
   Wrangel: Eh man überhaupt dran denkt, Herr Fürst! (*Tod*, I, v.)
   Gräfin: Nur in Entwürfen bist du tapfer, feig
              In Thaten. (*Tod*, I, vii.)

words not only from his own lips but from those of the Dovre King, the Lean One, and the Button-Moulder.[27]

The charges, then, which Hamlet brings against himself are not, though they might well be, confirmed or substantiated. Instead, the evidence points the other way. In addition to what we have already considered, there is the fact that the two soliloquies of self-reproach are so contrived as to end each in a definite resolve, and that a resolve which is kept. "The play's the thing," in the one case; "From this time forth my thoughts be bloody or be nothing worth," in the other. Both times Hamlet, upon consideration, mends his ways: he turns from his sin of inaction, and his repentance is unto life. But the action he resolves on, you say, is not to the point—not revenge. You say this, however, because you are a critic, or a psychologist; or because you have read others' criticisms of the play; or because you have read the play more than you have seen it. In both cases it is action, not collapse; in both cases it is action which has to do with the King and with thwarting him; what is more, in both cases it is action which wholly satisfies the speaker himself. After the second soliloquy he complains of himself, questions himself, no more. And that the audience will observe, and are meant to observe, much more readily than the circumstance that the action is not the supreme one of killing the King. So the dramatist is enabled to content his audience, shield his hero, and still prolong his play.

6

Why, then, if such be the poet's intention, does he drop out of consideration two details found both in the *Fratricide Punished* and in Belleforest, and therefore probably in Kyd himself? I mean the guards or multitude of courtiers who make the King's person inaccessible to Hamlet, and Hamlet's avowal that he feigned madness as a device to reach him.[28] It has been thought that Shakespeare's omission of these two bits of external motivation looked as if he meant really to ground the delay in Hamlet's character. But as used by Kyd they had probably been stop-gaps and nothing more. In the *Fratricide Punished* they rest on two simple assertions of the hero. The German Hamlet twice speaks of the guards hindering his approach to the King, and that is all. The hindrance is not represented directly—that is, dramatically,—and the hero makes no effort, and lays no plan, to outwit or circumvent the guards. In Alfieri's *Oreste*

---

[27] Both plays are pieces of symbolism. But the symbolists' methods seem to be about the only ones nowadays whereby these indefinable matters can effectively be brought upon the stage. Warranted by this convention, concreteness and explicitness do not offend.

[28] *F.P.* II, v: My worthy friend Horatio, through this assumed madness I hope to get the opportunity of revenging my father's death. You know, however, that my father [his uncle, the King] is always surrounded by many guards; wherefore it may miscarry.

V, i: Hither have I come once more, but cannot attain to my revenge because the fratricide is surrounded all the time by so many people.

and, in less measure, in Euripides' play on the same subject, the *Electra*, we see the difference: there Egisthus is surrounded with satellites or guards, but their brute force is met by stratagem and cunning. This helps make the story; it gives the revenger something appropriate and relevant to do. Of this there is nothing in the *Fratricide Punished;* and if there was anything in the old *Hamlet* it probably furnished about as primitive and unconvincing a dramatic situation as the corresponding motive of retardation in the *Spanish Tragedy*, where Hieronimo is hindered in his suit for justice to the King. He is "borne down" by Lorenzo's "nobilitie." "The King sees me," he says, "and faine would heare my sute. Why, is not this a strange and seld-seene thing?" he asks (and any one would agree with him) "that standers by with toyes [trifles] should strike me mute?"[29] The hero's statement concerning the hindrance comes to nothing; the motivation is a makeshift, is really a pretence. So with the feigned madness as a passport to the King's presence or a means of facilitating the revenge.[30] Nothing comes of that, either; indeed, in Belleforest and the *Fratricide Punished*, as in *Hamlet*, the madness has, if anything, quite the opposite result. The two bits of motivation,[31] then, are, as they stand, flimsy and nugatory; to make them otherwise Shakespeare would have had to contrive an intrigue of his own, instead of adopting Kyd's; and since such motiving does not explain but only calls attention to the need of explanation, he shrewdly holds his péace. Your dramatic artist, like Sir Robert Walpole, who by virtue of his office of Prime Minister was something of a dramatic artist too, lets sleeping dogs lie.

Instead of enhancing the reputation of the hero, indeed, these two bits of motivation, if anything, impair it. The double implication is that he is not clever, and that he is chary of adventure and careful for his life. In Belleforest the hero avows to his mother that he feigns madness and procrastinates for his own safety. And when Hieronimo receives the letter from Belimperia, disclosing the identity of the murderers, he cries,

> Hieronimo, beware, thou art betraide
> And to entrap thy life this traine is laide.
> Aduise, thee, therefore, be not credulous:
> This is deuised to endanger thee . . .

Prudent and sensible this is, but not dashing. But Shakespeare's heroic figures are commonly, I will not say beyond, but a little above, the con-

---

[29] III, xii, 64-82. Cf. xii, 2-4; xiv, 53-56.

[30] Cf. above, p. 25, note 28.

[31] Besides these, here omitted, there may have been another. In both Belleforest and the *Fratricide Punished*, (I, vi) the hero avows the intention to secure a vengeance for ever memorable ("qu'il en sera à iamais parlé en ces terres," Evans, p. 14). If this appeared in the old *Hamlet* it was little in accord, to be sure, with the course of the plot. In Belleforest the hero plans the scene of slaughter at the end; but in all versions of *Hamlet*, as in the *Fratricide Punished*, the King does the planning and Hamlet is taken off his guard.

siderations of prudence and common sense; careless and reckless of their lives, as are Hotspur, Romeo and Mercutio, Brutus, Antony, and Coriolanus; and it is interesting to see that Shakespeare would have Hamlet rank with these. He holds his life at a pin's fee at the beginning, and he holds it no higher at the end. And that is another reason for Shakespeare's avoiding the subject of danger. In his self-reproaches Hamlet calls himself a coward; by his conduct, therefore, he must furnish not the slightest justification for the charge.

7

The technique, then, the similarity of the technique to that in other Shakespearean and Elizabethan plays and to what we can learn of that in the old play, the unanimous testimony of the two centuries nearest the poet,—all these things conspire together to prove that Hamlet was meant to be an ideal character. He has no tragic fault, any more than has Romeo—like Romeo's his fault is not in himself but in his stars. And thus conceived, he seems much more Shakespearean and Elizabethan—being less Coleridgean and German. As conceived by the Romanticists he is an anomaly—unlike any other character of the time. He was an innovation of genius, maybe; but, if such, he made no stir in the world and called forth no imitation. There are other revenge tragedies after *Hamlet*, but no weak or irresolute revenger. Tourneur follows Marston, who provides his revenger with plenty to do. And Shakespeare himself never before or after created a character like him—if such he be. But alike are his other tragic heroes. However under Senecan and Renaissance influence they may bewail themselves, all are quick and gallant spirits. Romeo, both before and after he lies on the ground with his own tears made drunk, shows the pluck of a paladin. Indeed, it is probable that a hero really actuated by craven scruples and reflective cowardice would, in those rough-and-ready times, have found small favor on the tragic stage. Comedy, the comedy of humours, was the place for him. And Richard II is no exception. He is taken from history, for one thing, the acts or events of which "have not that magnitude which satisfieth the mind of man." Unlike Hamlet, moreover, he is not praised in the play or in any way held up to admiration. The worthy and serious-minded all pity him or condemn him. But even he is not irresolute. Like Marlowe's Edward, he is made fickle and capricious, easily uplifted and as easily cast down, but not irresolute. The fluctuations of Edward's or Richard's passion, which make the situations, are of a different order; the passions themselves are frivolous or terrible, as they come and go; but there is about them nothing pusillanimous or feeble. Neither Edward nor Richard is so tame and weak as to evade or procrastinate. They rush to extremes, instead. There is no great duty from before the face of which they shrink and shy

away.   Duties, indeed, do not trouble them.   But it is a sign of the health
and noble simplicity of the Elizabethans that nowhere in their serious
drama, so far as I am aware, is there a good character who, confronted by
his duty, fails to face it.   By the *maladie du siècle*, the malady of a later
age—the age of Werther, Coleridge, and Sénancour, in which our Hamlet really had his birth—they are untouched.

So far are Shakespeare's other heroes removed from the infection that
they are, all of them, great of heart, bold in deed, even strong and lithe of
limb, as today no hero need be.   They are worthies, champions, tall men of
their hands.   Othello, as he bids his uncle let him come forth, cries, "I have
made my way through more than twenty times your stop"; old Lear, in his
last hours, kills Cordelia's executioner; Macbeth, Antony, and Coriolanus
perform prodigies of valour single-handed in the field.   And just such, we have
seen, is Hamlet.   He dauntlessly follows the Ghost; he welcomes the perilous sport of the expedition to England; and when pitted against them
hand to hand, he is more than a match for his antagonists,—whether
struggling on the platform, killing the spy in the bedchamber, boarding
the pirate ship, grappling in the grave, or fencing and stabbing and wrest-
ing the cup at the end.   These are the "acts and events greater and more
heroical," which in tragedy Elizabethan dramatic taste required.   Indeed,
the dramatist seems to have deliberately suppressed or avoided much of
what might remind us of the student or scholar.   The original Hamlet,
probably, was as pedantic, and talked as much Latin, as old Hieronimo.
In Quarto 1 he appears twice with a book in his hand, in Quarto 2 but
once.   And Hamlet once seems to make a distinction, and speaks to Horatio
of "your philosophy" as if it were he that was the student rather than
himself.[32]   No one calls him a scholar save Ophelia, who at the same time
calls him a courtier and soldier; and no one scorns him or condescends to
him, we have seen, as a bookish, dreamy, impractical person, though one
might expect the King, Polonius, or at least Laertes to do it.   He is
a student of the Renaissance, taking to his sword as readily as to his ink-
horn and book,—indeed in all Shakespeare who takes to his sword more
readily?   Even before the slaughter at the end, Hamlet might well have
rubbed his eyes and cried out with Candide: "Hélas! mon Dieu! je suis
le meilleur homme du monde et voilà déjà trois hommes que je tue."   And
at the end, though he envies Laertes his reputation as a fencer, he awaits
the combat with confidence—a confidence fully warranted by the event.
"You will lose this wager, my lord"—"I do not think so . .   I shall win
at the odds."   He does better than that—he has more "hits" to his credit
than Laertes—and, when what began in play ends up in grim earnest, he has
killed two enemies, to their one.   Why should a dreamy weakling, a melan-

[32] It is possible, of course, to take "your" in its peculiar indefinite sense.

choly doubter or cynic, one broken in will or hopelessly engulfed in thought, be made so healthy and sturdy—so formidable—a man of this world?

Now Shakespeare is, in his method, emphatic and unmistakable; and if he had suddenly resolved to abandon heroic romance, and undertake a novel—a psychological—type of character, such as Hamlet has, in the last century, been understood to be, he would have tried to make him as different as possible from his other characters—make him really a Werther, an Aprile, or, say, a Romeo who kept his sword like a dancer and shunned danger and death. Instead, he has, save for the delay, given him all the stout qualities of the others. Instead, he has kept for him all the stout qualities he had had in Kyd. How, then, could an audience detect the difference, if a difference there was meant to be? And to indicate a difference that the audience could not detect, Shakespeare, of course, was not the man to have lifted a finger. He was not painting pictures that were never to be seen, not shooting arrows into the air. He was writing plays which plain and common people were expected to like, and in order to like them, of course, must understand. How naturally—and how differently from us—they understood the play now in question we have learned already.

CHAPTER III

THE CHANGES IN QUARTO 2 AND THE REASON FOR THEM

So far we have been viewing the version of Quarto 2 and the Folio mainly in relation to the old *Hamlet*, as we learn of this last through other sources. What now of Quarto 2 and the Folio, in relation to Quarto 1? It matters not greatly, in this connection, how much of Quarto 1 is Kyd or how much Shakespeare, for it is the changes that reveal the dramatist's purpose. Quarto 1, to be sure, being incomplete and mutilated, is only a surreptitious and second-hand report of Shakespeare's first version. Not much can be made, therefore, of the absence or omission in Quarto 1— particularly in the more abbreviated latter half of it—of what we find in Quarto 2 and the Folio. It is otherwise with omissions and positive modifications, in Quarto 2 and the Folio, of the material to be found in Quarto 1. These, on the whole, make for a more compact, a more vividly interesting play. Such was the dramatist's intention, no doubt, though in the process he has not made it a more coherent and consistent play. For the student, as we shall see, if not for the playgoer, an element of confusion and obscurity is produced as a result of shifting and omitting scenes and of toning down Kyd's crudities. All this affects character; but the improving and subtilizing of the characterization of the hero was not, I think, the chief thought of the dramatist. That result he secured mainly by transmuting the dross of Kyd's bombast into the gold of Hamlet's lines. Neither there, however, nor in the matters of structure and incident, which we are considering, are there changes which, so far as I can discover, were necessarily prompted by an intent to indicate a weakness in the hero. Some of them, on the contrary, lend him greater dignity and a nobler pathos. Yet the dramatist's chief thought was not of that but (as it should be) of the play as a whole.

1

The most remarkable change is the shifting of the "To be or not to be" soliloquy from Act II into Act III,—to a point after Hamlet has resolved on the play to catch the conscience of the King. Critics who have not laid this at the door of the reporter,[1] have, so far as I am aware, drawn the inference that here is pragmatic proof of Shakespeare's intention to show Hamlet's utter inability to keep to the issue in hand. It puts the official seal and sanction upon the Coleridgean criticism. He meditates on killing oneself[2]—God save the mark!—when hot on the trail of the man he is to kill! And that establishes them in their belief that Hamlet's

---

[1] For this unjustifiable position see above, p. 2, note 3, and below, p. 36, note 13.

[2] Not himself, of course; it is the subject of suicide in general. See below, p. 36.

project is a pretext or subterfuge, and that he undertakes the play, whether he knows it or not, to put off doing his duty.

In Quarto 1 the soliloquy in question stands early in the second act, and immediately follows Polonius' report to the King that Hamlet is mad for love of his daughter. But, as in Quarto 2, it is directly connected with the scene in which Hamlet bids Ophelia "get her to a nunnery." At the moment Polonius has finished his story, the King espies Hamlet at hand "poring upon a book." Polonius seizes the opportunity, gets rid of the Queen, stations Ophelia aloof, where she shall not at once be noticed, —with a book in her hand, too, as a pretext for her presence there in the gallery,—and bestows the King and himself behind the arras. Just so it is in Quarto 2, save that now Hamlet has no book. In either version, then, the soliloquy, which originally arose out of the train of thought suggested by his reading, and its accompanying mood of mental abstraction, provides Hamlet with something to do while these arrangements are making, and until his eyes shall light on the girl. It is a convenient means of making his unsuspicion plausible; it stands attached, therefore, to the nunnery scene rather than the nunnery scene to it. So we shall consider the reason for shifting the nunnery scene as the fundamental subject of inquiry. In Quarto 1 this scene is in content the same as in Quarto 2, but the upshot is different. The King pooh-poohs Polonius' explanation of the madness as in the later version; but he does not apparently take alarm, and says not a word of sending the Prince to England.

Now, by shifting, in his later version, the nunnery scene, and the soliloquy which attaches to it, into Act III, Shakespeare obtained effects of suspense and of climax. Instead of having the principal attempt to pluck out the heart of Hamlet's mystery undertaken as soon as it is determined on, immediately after Polonius' disclosure, he lets intervene the two minor attempts—Polonius' own, single-handed, and Rosencrantz and Guildenstern's. Thus Polonius learns nothing; thus Rosencrantz and Guildenstern learn next to nothing; and naturally the King's suspicions lead him at last to take a hand himself. In the nunnery scene in either position, moreover, whether in Quarto 1 or Quarto 2, Hamlet, intentionally or unintentionally, betrays himself ("all that are married but one shall live"); but only in the later position, in Quarto 2, was it possible for the dramatist to give this self-betrayal full effect in the King's alarm. Polonius and Rosencrantz and Guildenstern might plausibly be set upon Hamlet by the King before he takes alarm but not afterward! And how much more dramatic and climactic is this arrangement, as, in Quarto 2, the King, roused when Polonius makes report, sets on Polonius, then sets on Rosencrantz and Guildenstern, and finally goes eavesdropping on his own account, to learn even more than he cared to know! Polonius' and Rosencrantz and Guildenstern's soundings seem meaningless and profitless except as they whet the King's appetite for more. By this arrangement, moreover, the nunnery scene, the great emotional scene of renunciation, moves nearer to the centre of action and passion—just before the play-within-the-play and the scene in the bedchamber. There they stand, in true Shakespearean fashion, with "scenes in lower key"—the talk with the Player and the raillery of Rosencrantz and Guildenstern—set, for relief, in between.

What heightens the effect of this change, moreover, is the interweaving of strands of the story, which is quite in Shakespeare's better manner. In Quarto 1 he no doubt follows Kyd: Polonius makes his report, Hamlet happens in all too opportunely for the occasion[3]—"pat he comes like the catastrophe in the old comedy,"—and at once the eavesdropping begins. In Quarto 2 Shakespeare has Polonius and the King arrange for such an experiment some time in the future, whenever they shall find Hamlet walking, as is his custom, there in the lobby alone; and thus we not only are saved an inartistic coincidence but also are prompted to sit up in our seats and await that moment. By the new arrangement we are invited, as an audience should be, to look ahead; and, at the same time, are not expected to believe that in real life occasions and opportunities come, as in a fairy-tale, at call, at the waving of a wand.

2

Another improvement due to interweaving is the placing of the nunnery scene almost immediately before the *Murder of Gonzago*, directly after the project of the play is launched. As a result the King comes to the performance, not indifferent, but in a state of suspicion and suppressed alarm. He knows that Hamlet has intentions on his life even though Hamlet may not know of his guilt; he has already resolved upon England, though not as yet upon another murder. By this position the play scene gains in intensity; just as does the nunnery scene itself, indeed, with its menace for the King and its pathos for Hamlet and Ophelia, now that Hamlet is already at a perilous and momentous stage of his enterprise of detection and revenge. In both cases the coming event casts its shadow before. "Get thee to a nunnery," has a sharper ring of anguish now that he is about to come to grips with this wickedness, which envelops the frail Ophelia and involves her. So with the soliloquy. "How much more significant," says Professor Lewis Campbell,[4] "is the calm utterance of deep melancholy and the poignant enforced interview with his lost love, awakening an agony of wounded affection and suspicion at the moment when the fateful issue was about to be determined, when the cardinal discovery was impending, and the need for crushing out 'all pressures past' was more than ever imperative in its demand."

---

[3] See below, p. 36, note 13.

[4] *Fortnightly Review*, v. 78, p. 508.

In all three cases the change has but turned story into drama. It is such a change as Shakespeare was many a time again to make and had made before. In Brooke's *Romeus and Juliet* the killing of Tybalt follows the wedding-night. In the play this dire event comes between it and the marriage. Thus the emotional, the dramatic, quality of the wedding-night is deepened. Banishment, Mantua, separation in the moment of their bliss, stares the young lovers in the face.

The change, then, makes for economy of means, compactness and richness of texture, and heightening of suspense and dramatic interest. And as for character? Hamlet is not the only character. The change heightens the impression of the intelligence of the King and raises up in him a more formidable antagonist. Quarto 1 is defective; but the fact remains that though he has just as much reason to do so,[5] the King does not take alarm after the nunnery scene, and neither then nor after the Mousetrap has a word to say of England, or any other word of fear or menace until after Polonius' death; nay, by setting on outsiders like Polonius and Rosencrantz and Guildenstern after the nunnery scene,[6] he shows either that he is not alarmed or is not sensible. But in Quarto 2 and the Folio he not only seems more intelligent and dangerous but he is constantly more aroused. Three times he there menaces his nephew with deportation—after the nunnery scene, after the Mousetrap, and after the death of Polonius; and each time the menace is less guarded, until at the end he fairly shows his teeth and sting. This lends import and progressive effect to that series of probings or soundings (both the King's and Hamlet's own) which begins with Polonius' conversation with Hamlet about his daughter and ends with the scene in the Queen's bedchamber, where, after the old busybody's ears are become deaf as dust, the truth about the Prince's madness is at last revealed. And so far as Hamlet himself is concerned, it is as if all the while a thunder cloud were rising behind his back, which, though we see it, he himself does not see until the end of the bedchamber scene—did not see, ironically enough, when he spared the King at prayer. Whether in plot or in character, consequently, the main result of the change is to pit the Prince and the King more evenly against each other, and to let us perceive more clearly through the gloom "the fell incensed points of mighty opposites." "Nearly all that has been

[5] In this scene in Quarto 1 Hamlet is just as evidently not mad for love, just as evidently "dangerous"; and he says the same thing about the married:—"all but one shall live."

[6] In Quarto 1 the King asks them almost the same questions, and gives them the same directions, as, in Quarto 2, he does *before* the nunnery scene. See III, i. Even in Quarto 2, to be sure, it is unplausible that the murderer should use deputies at all to discover the cause of the madness of his victim's son. That is the old story of Belleforest; but in it what the murderer wanted was to know whether the madness was genuine. Relatively, however,—and that is all we are considering—Shakespeare's change is an improvement. It is also unplausible in Quarto 2, as in Quarto 1, that the King should allow the Queen to sound the Prince, and Polonius to listen; but this is Polonius' doing, not the King's, and there is not the danger in their knowledge that there is in Rosencrantz and Guildenstern's.

written of the play," as Professor Kittredge has recently noted, "has been out of focus; it is the tragedy, not of an individual, but of a group; and in its structure it is balanced in the most delicate and unstable equilibrium between two great personages, Hamlet and the King."[7] This view of the play is in keeping with Horatio's final comment as he addresses Fortinbras, as well as with the earliest criticism, such as that in *Some Remarks* from which we quoted above, and the still earlier one of James Drake, in 1699, to which we have already alluded and which we take up again below.[8] It is especially in keeping with the changes introduced in connection with the nunnery scene.

3

To this scene, as I have shown, the celebrated soliloquy is directly attached. It serves to introduce the scene—to furnish Hamlet with something to do and think about as he comes into the lobby, and to cover the eavesdroppers' retreat. For the stage-craft the soliloquy was needed in its new position in Quarto 2 just as in the old; and consequently it was shifted too. But that is not the view the critics have taken, being concerned more about stage-craft than character. What strange meditations, they say (and they have said it since the days of Coleridge), when business of such moment is afoot! There is the dreamer, again, all adrift! What, then, would they have him talk about? one wonders. Of his play and the acting of it? That he discusses with the actor in the ensuing scene. Of the King and his revenge, of his private griefs and shortcomings? Yes, that he should do—if his part in the play were, as people are inclined to think, the mere portrait or embodiment of a soul, and every phrase were a trait. But if it be but a play, a story not of one but of many persons on the stage, what of the two fellows behind the arras? Hamlet is soliloquizing; but, when eavesdroppers are at hand for the purpose, soliloquies on the Elizabethan stage are overheard. A pretty plight for the dramatist—a prettier plight for his hero—if he let Hamlet speak out now his whole mind, as, to preserve his reputation for a practical man, people would have him do. The notion of a practical man entertained by Elizabethan spectators was just the contrary, and so far at least as cleverness and cunning was concerned, Hamlet was such a man. As in

[7] *Shakespeare* (1916), p. 40. But as for the balancing and equilibrium, one must a little demur, or at least make reservations. Certainly Hamlet thwarts and checkmates the King in his moves; but Hamlet himself is not thwarted—never moves. He only makes ready to do so, as in the play-within-the-play and in drawing his sword on the King at prayer. "Claudius," says Professor Kittredge, referring to current criticism, "is belittled . . . and Hamlet's real obstacle being thus cleared from his path—a new obstacle is called into being to account for his delay; namely, a complete misrepresentation of his mental and moral character." As to the latter statement there can be no question; but if in his brief summary Professor Kittredge would convey that it is the King that thwarts Hamlet's efforts I do not see the evidence for his view. There is in the text no intimation of which I am aware that Hamlet cannot at any time gain access to the King and stab him. Where would be the Hamlet problem, if there were?

[8] P. 64.

Belleforest, he plays the King's game but always beats him at it. He is never quite cornered, never caught asleep. If he is not permitted to know the King's purposes, he sees a "cherub that sees them." Whether he knows them this time or does not know them, this is a trap—have the spectators not seen Polonius and the King set it?—and Heaven keep the young Prince out of its teeth! They start up in their seats, we may be sure, when he takes his cue. And when his speech turns out to be only a philosophical discourse and reverie they will not hold its unbusinesslike character up against him, I judge, since he proves so sensible as not to speak of his private business where walls have ears. They are on pins and needles lest he may speak of it, if they are an audience worth having.

Nor are the vagueness and irrelevance of the details, as has been thought, to be reckoned against him. He speaks of the oppressor's wrong, the proud man's contumely, the law's delay, the insolence of office, from all of which he himself cannot have suffered, and the undiscovered country from whose bourn no traveler returns, though one had just returned to him. But as for this last, how in that country itself the myriad-minded one must now sit and smile as he watches the commentators ponder—or make capital of—the phrase! It is no symptom of skepticism. It is to be taken naturally, as all expressions in Shakespeare are to be taken, without too far-reaching a regard for context, without a thought of the Ghost.[9] It is a rare old saying, changed a bit but without really dramatic modification:

unde non unquam remeavit ullus,[10]

or, as Caxton has it, "from which I sawe never man come agayn." It is an unguarded word, such as we find not in Ibsen, or for which, if we found it, our present-day precise artistic conscience would call him to account. And that here and in the soliloquy in general the commentators catch Hamlet up and cavil at his irrelevance is simply due to their failure to appreciate the looseness of Elizabethan dramatic structure. They expect unity, close communion between all the elements of expression in the play; they would have their dramatic characters speak with regard to the company, duly mindful of every circumstance, and by the card. Consequently they find that Hamlet here is meant to be either doubting or rambling; or else, in order to make him speak more strictly to the question, they wrest his words. Some critics, accordingly, adopt Johnson's interpretation (though long ago refuted by Malone) that Hamlet is meditating,

---

[9] It is refreshing when a commentator can take it so, as does Dr. Furness: "Is it not evident that Shakespeare is speaking in his own person?"

[10] *Herc. Œt.*, l. 1527. Cf. *Herc. Furens*, l. 865:

unde numquam
Cum semel venit potuit reverti.

not on suicide, but on revenge and the consequences of revenge.[11] It is a pity for clearness' sake that in making the change from Quarto 1 Shakespeare could not also have transferred the business of "reading on a book."[12] He kept it in Act II as a point of departure for the talk with Polonius— "words, words," "slanders"—and it could not be repeated here. Ophelia is here reading already, and for both to be reading when they meet, as in Quarto 1, no doubt seemed to him ridiculous. But the chief reason is that Hamlet would then a second time come reading on the stage. That would be to make a bookworm of him—and to play into the hands of critics yet unborn. That would be to make Hamlet "Germany" after all. Reading, however, not the fulness of his heart, it is well to remember, was the original motive, or occasion, of his discourse. And this is only one of many changes whereby, in seeking effectiveness, the dramatist has slightly ruptured the continuity of his story.[13]

Soliloquies couched in general and somewhat impersonal form are common enough. In Shakespeare himself there are Henry IV's soliloquy on sleep and Henry V's on ceremony. What is more remarkable is speeches addressed to others, but so wide the strictly dramatic mark as Mercutio's on Queen Mab and Jaques' "All the world's a stage," or that death's-head meditation in *Measure for Measure* imparted to Claudio by the Duke disguised as a friar. In delivering these it has always been the custom of the stage for the speaker to ignore the other characters, even turn his back on them. And this the text warrants. The Duke keeps to his rôle of moralizing friar, but what he says is cast in gnomic form,

[11] Lewis (*Genesis of Hamlet*, p. 100) does this.

[12] See Act II, ii, 168: "*Enter Hamlet reading on a book.* Queen: But look where sadly the poor wretch comes reading."

[13] From the foregoing considerations it would appear that, as in Quarto 1, the nunnery scene and soliloquy must have stood in this place in Act II in the original *Hamlet;* and that Quarto 1 is not, as Professor Creizenach insists, a corruption of Quarto 2. (See above, p. 2, note 3, especially the reference to the *Library*.) Not only does the evidence of the *Fratricide Punished* (II, iv) point in this direction, but the general character of Kyd's art (or of pre-Shakespearean art) as well. Preparations, and interlacings with climactic effect, had not yet arrived; patness of coincidence was not objectionable. Just as in Quarto 1 the experiment follows promptly upon the heels of the proposal, so in the *Spanish Tragedy*, I, iv, Lorenzo having proposed that they spend the time in sports and revelling, Horatio cries: "The King, my lords, is coming hither straight, To feast the Portingall Embassadors"; and forthwith (sc. v) the revelling begins. So the plan of Hieronimo's play-within-the-play is hatched with Belimperia immediately after her reproaches; in come his enemies who are destined to play, to deadly purpose, their parts in it, and the old fellow invites them, and "fits" them on the spot. This is all in one scene, IV, i; and only Isabella's final soliloquy intervenes between that and the performance. Besides, there is evidence in Quarto 2, as we have just seen, of dislocation. (Cf. also Lewis, *Genesis*, pp. 23-28.) The natural thing, one feels inclined to add, would be to put Polonius' theory to the test (his daughter being at hand) at once; and this cannot be done without the King to witness it. The theory having failed him, it would be the natural thing, again, for Polonius to sound Hamlet anew. To be sure, Ophelia is not present in Act II, Sc. 2 of Quarto 2; but that she was present in the original version, as in Quarto 1, is apparent. At II, i, 118 Shakespeare has kept the expression "goe we to the King" (Quarto 1: "Lets to the King"). That she does not reappear with her father is due to Shakespeare's postponing the experiment of the nunnery scene to Act III; and to the further consideration that it is more seemly that Ophelia should not be present, to be embarrassed by her father's asinine deportment, the Queen's rebuke, and the discussion of her own love affairs.

addressed to anybody. And speaking to a young man, father of a babe in arms whose too precipitate appearance has been the cause of present difficulties, he seems as forgetful of recent momentous events as is Hamlet himself:

> For thine own bowels, which do call thee sire,
> The mere effusion of thy proper loins,
> Do curse the gout, serpigo, and the rheum
> For ending thee no sooner.

Nor is this irrelevance and impersonality in meditation at all confined to Shakespeare; indeed Hamlet's talk here, and in the graveyard, is probably, along with other matters in the play, influenced by Marston's *Malcontent* (1600).[14] Neither is it confined to the Elizabethan age. It is not lacking in Calderon and in the Greeks. There is Hippolytus's long tirade on the wickedness of woman,—on the misfortune that there should be such a creature, whom fathers are glad to get rid of and husbands must then have on their hands.[15] And there are the choruses, often so general that commentators are at some pains to trace the connection, such as that at line 944 of the *Antigone*, on Danae, Cleopatra, and Lycurgus, the first two innocent and the last guilty, the only similarity of whom to Antigone lies in "their noble birth and their cruel imprisonment."[16] In Greek, Senecan, and Elizabethan tragedy alike, moreover, there are numerous choruses, speeches, and soliloquies which manifest not only the generalizing but a moralizing tendency.[17] The Greek choruses of this description would fit almost any tragedy as well as that in which they occur. They dilate on Man's ignorance of his fate, his insolence and rashness, the folly of calling him happy before death, the fickleness of fortune, the irrefragable power of Zeus and his laws. This, on a large scale, is only what on a small scale occurs throughout—in the *sententiae*, which abound particularly in classical tragedy, but which, in more flexible and less isolated form, are not infrequent in Shakespeare's maturest work. The evolution—the differentiation—was, in his day, not complete. Not every thought that Shakespeare put into a play was fused and transmuted into the essential substance of drama.

4

Another change in Quarto 2 is the addition of the last soliloquy, "How all occasions do inform against me." Its absence in Quarto 1 as it stands proves, of course, nothing; but since the presence of the soliloquy in Quarto

---

[14] See below, pp. 72-73, note 4, and my article "Hamlet, Marston, and the Malcontent Type," *Modern Philology* (1906), especially pp. 300-301.

[15] Ll. 616-67.

[16] Jebb, *ad loc.*

[17] For these in Elizabethan tragedy see Prof. M. L. Arnold's *Soliloquies of Shakespeare* (1911), pp. 149-54.

2 has generally been taken to indicate Shakespeare's intention to present a procrastinating character, we need concern ourselves only to show that, if added it was, Shakespeare had not that purpose but another.

In this soliloquy a contrast is established between Hamlet and Fortinbras, as in the earlier soliloquy there was one between him and the Player.[18] In either case there is not much of a parallel; but Hamlet's sensitive young spirit finds one, and is overcome with shame. In real life, to our experience of which the critics are always appealing, would a reproach on such an occasion discredit him? And when it comes to the charges, we have already seen how vaguely Hamlet speaks when he brings them, how he then puts them from him, shakes his head, and says he "does not know." But his ignorance is not that of skepticism, bewildered impotence, or despair. He does not know the reason, for there is no reason, and there is nothing for it but to make an end:

> O from this time forth
> My thoughts be bloody or be nothing worth.

The resolve, as I showed above, is kept. Rosencrantz and Guildenstern are sent packing into eternity, the pirate ship is boarded, and Hamlet presently returns, after defying the King in a letter, to have it out with him. And never again, as we have seen, does he complain or reproach himself: instead, he speaks, on his return, of the impending deed as if there were no question about it and had never been any. "Is't not perfect conscience?" he asks Horatio, "to quit him with this arm?" And when he replies that news of the death of the two courtiers will soon be reaching the King, Hamlet rejoins, "It will be, short; the interim is mine." Such accents (unless we be utterly dead and insensible to the finer shades of language, and to the characteristic intonations of human speech) are not meant for those either

---

[18] It is by these contrasts that Shakespeare designs to cast reflections upon Hamlet, not by that with Laertes. And both are so arranged that they throw no harsh light upon him, except in Hamlet's own eyes. His generous envy does him honor. With Laertes there is parallelism in the matter of losing a father—no more,—and Hamlet, again, in words like Hieronimo's to Bazulto (III, xiii, 161), is the one to recognize it: "For by the image of my cause, I see the portraiture of his." The contrast between them, however, is favorable; it is such a contrast as between Edgar and Edmund, Cordelia and Regan, Banquo and Macbeth. Laertes' promptitude is a minor matter, and, considering his recklessness of right and wrong, not greatly to his credit. Better delay with Hamlet, Shakespeare, if questioned, would have answered, than strike in the dark with Laertes. But modern criticism turns this round, as if the play were the *Statue and the Bust*, though without that comment which even in the nineteenth century a Browning thought it necessary to add:

> Oh, a crime will do
> As well, I reply, to serve for a test
> As a virtue golden through and through.

Shakespeare's contrasts are moral rather than psychological; the critics make them psychological rather than moral. It is only what they do, though, to his characters in general. If they would but consider how Shakespeare reversed the process in making them! In his sources he had warrant for making Richard III and Macbeth, though bad men, good kings. He deliberately made them bad kings. Think of Browning or Balzac doing it! He deliberately avoided this psychological complication, then new to the stage, to attain imaginative simplicity and moral intensity and impressiveness. (See on Laertes also Kittredge, *Shak.*, p. 39.)

of irresolution or of evasion. How calm he is, how steady! His teeth are not set nor are his nerves on a tension, for he has known no failure and expects none. The hours of enforced deliquium and eclipse are over, and Hamlet is himself again—is really what he has always been.

Now the psychological theory implies a weakness not to be cured by finally coming to oneself or pulling oneself together; the genuine tragic fault loses its tragic quality and impressiveness if it be remedied in Act IV, before the catastrophe which it is supposed to bring about. But here that is not the question; and by adding this soliloquy Shakespeare shows still more clearly than elsewhere that Hamlet's tardiness is not a sin or a disease, not a taint in the blood or a clot on the brain, but simply, as he says, a case of remissness, forgetting, or neglect. And the neglect and delay are now over and done with: the soliloquy, with its final resolution, is there, if for nothing else, to show it. It is unthinkable, otherwise, that Hamlet should never, in the two acts which follow, utter a word of complaint or self-reproach again. Evidently the soliloquy was put in, not as an indictment, but to make clear what was the trouble, and end it. In the soliloquy at the close of Act II he had reproached himself with the duty undone, and, a doubt of the Ghost arising, he had resolved upon the play to catch the King. In this soliloquy he finds that still for some reason the duty is undone, and resolves on bloody deeds. "Thoughts," to be sure, is what he says; but that does not much matter since these are thoughts that bring deeds in their trail. In both soliloquies his words are made good; both soliloquies are—though not as they have hitherto been thought to be—landmarks in the drama.

Critics generally have taken a very different view of the matter, and have here found Hamlet particularly futile and impotent, boldly speaking of bloody deeds at the very moment when he goes to England without a murmur.[19] It is worse, they think, even than soliloquizing on "To be or not to be" after the scent is caught and the hunt is up. But is it not strange to make much of his failure to resist the royal order? He is in custody; and a man is not considered feeble or incapable because he does not fight the police when he is arrested, or because, though guiltless, he steps up to the scaffold without being driven or dragged. Acquiescence on such occasions is taken for granted; but here it is not altogether taken for granted. "I must to England," he had said to the Queen, "you know that." Thought of resistance does not occur to Hamlet or the dramatist either; but that he is not acquiescing impotently the dramatist has taken pains

---

[19] Cf. even Professor Lewis, for instance, p. 31: "Hamlet utters his strongest expression of resolute vindictiveness just as he is turning his back upon his task, perhaps for ever." But he is not turning his back, in reality. Nor is he, as Coleridge says (*Lect. on Shak.*, Bohn Ed., 1900, p. 164), giving himself up to his destiny, and hopelessly placing himself in the power and at the mercy of his enemies.

to make clear.   Hamlet falls in with his deportation only as part of his plan.
In Quarto 2 some lines are added to the bedchamber scene to show it.[20]

> *Ham.*   I must to England; you know that?
> *Queen.*   Alack,
> I had forgot. 'Tis so concluded on.
> *Ham.*   There's letters seal'd, and my two school-fellows,
> Whom I will trust as I will adders fang'd,
> They bear the mandate. They must sweep my way
> And marshal me to knavery. Let it work;
> For 'tis the sport to have the enginer
> Hoist with his own petar; and 't shall go hard
> But I will delve one yard below their mines,
> And blow them at the moon. O 'tis most sweet
> When in one line two crafts directly meet.

The language of futility or impotence indeed!   If it was the principle
of the plot, as of the story of Belleforest, for Hamlet to play the King's
game and beat him at it, then to go to England, or to start for England,
was but to play the game.   And the three matters which hang together—
the last soliloquy, these words before it about hoisting with the petar, and
the incident of the pirate capture in which Hamlet takes his fate into his
own hands and cuts loose from his companions, instead of being, without
a reason, set by his companions ashore,—all have been inserted into Quarto
2, as Professor Lewis suggests, to give to Hamlet's inaction the most favorable color.[21]   They show that at this critical moment he has not forgotten
the duty of the morrow, that indeed he is ready for the business of today.

5

His inaction is thought due to the fact that he dissipates the energy
of his resolve in an endless brooding on the deed required.[22]   I find, on the
contrary, that he is kept off that subject as much as may be.   In Act II
there is not a word of it save in the final soliloquy; in Act III not a word
save where he catches the King at prayer and where the Ghost appears;
in Act IV not a word save in the final soliloquy again; and in Act V not
a word save "Is't not perfect conscience?" and the rest.   Whether in the
soliloquies, moreover, or in talking to Horatio, Hamlet hardly uses the
word revenge or makes definite references to the impending deed.   Kyd's

---

[20] That they were not in the original, unmutilated Quarto 1, is made likely by the fact that in this
version as we have it the King himself says nothing of England, whether after the nunnery scene or after
the Mousetrap, as he does in Quarto 2.   Mere mutilation is not consistent, and would not explain the drop-
ping out of these things that hold naturally together.   Moreover, it is pretty clear that in the older version
there was a sharp ironical peripeteia in the bedchamber scene.   Hamlet thwarts the King's purpose in
spying, and wins over the Queen as a confidante, but by killing Polonius he brings about, at the height of
his success, his own deportation to England.   In Quarto 2 England has already been resolved upon.

[21] *Genesis of Hamlet*, pp. 31-34.

[22] Bradley, p. 106.   Bulthaupt (*op. cit.*, p. 305) thinks that Hamlet sets out for England to gain time
for reflection.   What he said before going, what he did when he went, alike seem not to matter.

Hamlet, in all likelihood, howled "Revenge!" or "Vindicta!" like Hieron-imo, Marston's Antonio, or, for that matter, the Ghost himself.[23]

Yet is not this very reticence a sign of the hero's indifference and in-capacity? And is not the author's evasion equivalent to the hero's? That would be like Hamlet's supposed irresponsibility in the "To be or not to be" soliloquy, or like his going to England when he ought to have stayed at home. By such negative means the author could avoid difficulties, but he could not convey to an audience that the hero was avoiding dif-ficulties. That is a positive effect, to be attained on the stage only by positive means. The author would then have had to cause his hero to say much and do little, to make plans and fail to carry them out, or else through his own confession or the comment of others conspicuously to appear to be avoiding the discussion of revenge or the making of plans which should lead to it. On the stage only the positive counts; the negative—silence or reticence, mere omission—goes unnoticed. Literary critics, who, in their subtlety, notice with pleasure little else, transpose drama into literature. And in this particular case reticence is really an example of the dramatist's practical finesse. Shakespeare again lets sleeping dogs lie—trusting to an interested audience not to notice it. They did not, we have seen, in two hundred years.

From plans, indeed, our dramatist shies away farther even than from the thought of revenge or the cause of the procrastination. Hamlet has no plans save for preliminaries, such as the feigned madness, the play, and the thwarting of the King in sending him to England—none for the deed itself. And it makes a particularly bad impression—I mean as a bit of reality, of course, not as art—that he produces no plan toward the end. Readers notice it, if spectators are too much engaged. But here Shakespeare is following his plot, no doubt, and is again stepping gingerly. The Prince is playing the King's game still, and reason for it. And if he loses in the psychological reader's respect he gains in the spectator's sym-pathy. For is it not a sorry business to scheme to catch a man and kill him? Setting traps, and, by deceit and cajolery, luring your victim into them, is not a hero's rôle. Agamemnon stepping blindly into the toils of his murderer makes a better play by far than Orestes and Pylades, in the various versions, hunting the murderer's trail. When, the year before, Shakespeare tried his hand at such an intrigue, as he followed Plutarch in *Julius Cæsar*, he by no means reached the summit of his art. Our sympathy goes out to the poor victim, despite all. And in the emotional

---

[23] Lodge, *Wits Miserie* (1596), p. 56, speaks of the pale "Visard of the ghost which cried so miserally at the Theator like an oister-wife, *Hamlet, reuenge.*" Dekker, *Satiromastix* (1602): "*Tucca.* My name's *Hamlet, reuenge;* thou hast been at Paris garden, hast thou not?" *Works* (1873) i, p. 229. *Westward Ho,* v. iii: "*Tenterhook.* Let these husbands play mad Hamlet, and crie reuenge." In Shakespeare's version Hamlet utters no such cry. Cf. also the later reference, Rowland's *Night Raven* (1620):

I will not cry, *Hamlet, Revenge* my greeves,
But I will call, *Hangman, Revenge* on theeves.—*Allusion-Book,* i, p. 157.

effect and tragic quality of his catastrophe he here gains immeasurably by letting the villain King still take the lead, and load his soul with the whole burden of the slaughter at the end. It is impossible, of course, that Hamlet should not suspect a fencing-match, arranged by his deadly enemy, with a man "whose hands but a few hours ago were at his throat." But it is impossible, also, as has been suggested, that he should suspect that the King and Laertes, reputed men of honor, would undertake to perpetrate such an outrage against the law of arms, in which success would mean infamy. Perhaps the improbabilities cancel each other; but, since the issue is not raised, the audience, in their absorption, actually think of neither. For Shakespeare the real and only question is how the tragedy shall remain a tragedy, and at the same time the hero act like the gallant gentleman he is and yet be not a fool. If Hamlet suspected, he would not enter the fight; or in case he did enter it, he would then be followed with less sympathy and anxiety, since he must needs come out ahead again, as the better man. By that the tragedy would be upset. Hamlet must perish, but neither falter nor fail. And in going to his death he keeps his reputation for astuteness as well as for reckless valor by giving utterance to a premonition, and with a smile defying it. Since he exhibits no plan, the reflective reader today may, with Professor Bradley, well shake his head at one so ready to die "with a sacred duty still undone"; but the unlettered audience is with him now more than ever, and joins in the judgment of audiences long ago at the Globe. If their point of view be taken (and what other are we entitled to take?) Shakespeare here again at the end has not been portraying the impotence of Hamlet's character but has been handling a situation, hedged about with difficulties, with consummate tact. He is presenting, not so much—in all its consistency—a character, as a highly emotional situation.

Throughout his later version he evades the subject of revenge, again, as by numerous minor omissions and substitutions, which we have not hitherto noticed, he secures the effect of Hamlet's secrecy. In Quarto 2 and the Folio no one is permitted to share the Ghost's revelations but Horatio, and he only late in the play. In the *Fratricide Punished* Horatio and Francisco learn immediately after the Ghost's disappearance that he has disclosed a horrible thing which craves vengeance; and after Francisco goes out Horatio is flatly told what it is. Both of these friends offer assistance but it is declined. There is nothing of this in Shakespeare. Hamlet has no confidant but Horatio, and except just before the Mousetrap he tells him nothing on the stage until late in Act V. What he does tell him implies in both cases previous confidences; but on the stage the only aspects of the situation touched upon are, in the first instance, the King's guilt, in the second, the justification of quitting him for it "with this arm." There is no word between them of revenge, until just when Hamlet is about to take it. We are not suffered to witness Hamlet's passionate confidences and vows of vengeance, or Horatio's sympathetic indignation and offers of aid. That, ordinarily, would make one of the great scenes, a *scène à faire*, perhaps; but here it would never do—we should then be expecting vengeance in the second act, or else a prolonged intrigue directed explicitly to that end. Two revengers, through four acts, could not well be kept from their business of revenge, if one could. Of Hamlet's purposes, indeed, there is until late in Act V no indication that Horatio is aware. In the *Fratricide Punished*, besides his disclosures in Act I Hamlet speaks to Horatio of his purpose of revenge both at the beginning of Act V and after the play, at the close of their discussion of the King's guilt. In Quarto 2 he does neither; and, as for the latter situation, it is pretty clear on comparison with Quarto 1 that for the best of reasons the dramatist gets rid of Horatio's embarrassing presence on the stage as soon as ever his work in helping detect the King's guilt is done.[24]

There is the same reticence with the Queen. In the *Fratricide Punished* the scene in the bedchamber is cut so short that it yields no evidence. But in Quarto 1 Hamlet speaks twice of revenge in her presence: once to the Ghost in words which in Quarto 2 and the Folio are replaced by vague and allusive language, and once to the Queen herself, in words which in Quarto 2 and the Folio are (surely by no chance) omitted. For in Quarto 1 the Queen is asked for assistance and promises it, whereas in Quarto 2 and the Folio she promises secrecy and no more. To do more she has no occasion, for she is not told[25] of Hamlet's purpose or even plainly given to understand that the former King was murdered.[26]

[24] There is no exit indicated for Horatio, but in both Quarto 2 and the Folio he says nothing after "I did very well note him" (l. 301). If he was meant to remain on the stage he is a quite idle spectator of Hamlet's mockery of Rosencrantz and Guildenstern and Polonius. Perhaps it is he who goes out at line 303 to call the Recorders. But in Quarto 1 Horatio stays on the stage to exchange another word—a simple and very foolish "goodnight"—at the end.

[25] The words "Murdered, damnably murdered," or their equivalent, in the description of the pictures, are omitted, as well as the repeated expressions of his purpose of "revenge." All that remains in Quarto 2 is: "As bad, good mother, as kill a king and marry with his brother." This is plain enough, you would think, but the Queen is permitted only to gasp at it. She is innocent, but Hamlet hits at the King over her shoulder.

[26] That in all these respects Quarto 1 represents the Kydian, or original, *Hamlet* appears from several circumstances. In the bedchamber scene in Belleforest the Queen is likewise told the whole truth and she promises her prayers. In *Antonio's Revenge* the same is the case, only it is after the bedchamber scene, for there Antonio speaks only to the Ghost. In that play and in the *Spanish Tragedy* the woman concerned is a confederate.

That the scene, as it stands in Quarto 1, is, though mutilated, not a corruption of that in Quarto 2, but an earlier version, is evident also from the structure of it. Though the character of the Queen is elevated, the scene in Quarto 2 loses in dramatic point. "But as the play was originally written," says Hunter (*Illustrations*, ii, p. 257), "the scene had a purpose. Hamlet reveals to his mother his knowledge of his uncle's guilt, and his purpose of revenge, and she engages to conceal and assist." What is more, there is here an ironical reversal. See above, p. 40 note 20. In Quarto 2 the scene is only the last step in a movement already started, and, in itself, presents a situation of great spiritual passion. But the sharpness of the reversal, or peripeteia, in Quarto 1 belongs to an earlier Shakespearean technique, and indeed to the technique of Kyd.

6

All this reticence and secrecy to what end?   Those who lean to psychology will hold that this again is Hamlet's evasion, and that he wants
no confidants because their knowledge would put him to shame.   But, if,
with Professor Bradley and most of the sounder critics, they be of the opinion
that he really desires to do the deed, though he cannot,[27] he would naturally
welcome confederates for the material support, and confidants for the moral.
He does not welcome them, or decline them, either.   Confederates like
Francisco and Horatio declined, confederates like the Queen and Horatio
welcomed but given no employment, and freer talk about revenge and his
purposes with them all,—this sort of thing, as in the *Fratricide Punished*
and Quarto 1, produces, in view of his delay, not a stronger but a weaker
impression of Hamlet's capacity.   And that, of all things, is the impression
that the dramatist is most anxious to avoid.

Not that this is the only purpose of these changes which make for
secrecy and reticence.   They also isolate the hero in his revenge; they
lend his revenge dignity and pathos.   Horatio is the direct descendant of
Pylades, as Hamlet is of Orestes; but Hamlet asks of him not the aid of
his sword or of his wits but only the consolation and refuge of his friendship.   The mandate was to the son alone; he is to quit the murderer "with
this arm" and not another's; and the poet would have the deed one not
of fealty but of filial love.   As confederates, Hamlet and Horatio would
leave us cold.   Our Hamlet cannot be suffered to stoop to ask any one for
help (or to receive it, either) in the doing of his duty.   In Kyd too, perhaps,
Horatio was only a confidant; but it is a considerable advantage, in the
circumstances, not to have the great secret imparted to him, as in Kyd
it probably was, on the stage.

And of equal advantage are these changes to the character of the Queen.
Dimly suspect as she may, she never learns of the murder; and while she
keeps the secret of Hamlet's sanity and his hatred of the King, she is not
disloyal to her lord.   This is in harmony with the loftier relation of love
and devotion between the adulterous pair which Shakespeare seems to
develop consistently in Quarto 2, and in Quarto 1, no doubt, had himself
originated.[28]   And the Queen is the more interesting for not having been
portrayed on the lines of the traditional adulterous mother; unlike Clytemnestra, she is true both to her wicked paramour and to her son.   With
ignorance, too, her conduct is more compatible in the rest of the play.   In
Quarto 1 she knows all, but afterwards she does not act as if she knew all:
she is asked for assistance, and promises it, but does nothing to keep her
promise.   In fact, despite her information and her promise, she after-

---

[27] That is, because of his infirmity, not because of external obstacles.

[28] Cf., for instance, IV, vii, 10-17, for which there is no equivalent in Quarto 1.

wards acts as she does in Quarto 2. But if the Queen wins favor in our
eyes through Hamlet's reticence, Hamlet wins still more.

>And, Mother, but assist mee in revenge,

he had said in Quarto 1,

>And in his death your infamy shall die.[29]

It is hardly the thing to ask your mother or your enemy's wife for help,
even though by so doing you give her a chance to wipe out her shame.[30]
It is as little romantic or heroic as old Hieronimo's (or Amleth's) fears
for his personal safety.[31]

[29] That this is not Shakespeare's style at this stage in his development, any one with an ear can tell. It is the primitive style and rhythm of a decade before.

[30] Nevertheless it has been reckoned against Hamlet that in Quarto 2 he here says nothing of revenge.

[31] See above, p. 26.

CHAPTER IV
THE HERO'S SELF-DECEPTION[1]

We have now viewed the play in its relations both to the old *Hamlet* and to Quarto 1. In the one case we saw that delay and reproaches for delay were not to be reckoned against the hero's character; both in the one case and in the other we saw how Shakespeare had thrust the subject of revenge into the background and slurred the delay over. It was Shakespeare, not Hamlet, who did this; but in showing that, we have hardly touched upon the problem of Hamlet's self-deception, which is supposed to be repeatedly involved. The critics, thinking him weak, irresolute, prone to stray off into the byways of thought, have taken the action in which he does engage for only a pretence at action, a futile substitute.

1

It is not to be wondered at that his feigning madness should be so taken, in view of the improbability of the venture (which we have already recognized[2]) in the circumstances. The antic disposition, they philosophically observe, is his "safety-valve." It is not so much deception as self-deception. But it was in the old play, and so must be in the new. Hamlet would not be Hamlet without it. Indeed it was too effective an artifice to dispense with—the high-spirited prince saying under his mask pretty much what he means, and yet misunderstood. By it he is spared the ignominy of playing the part of flatterer or friend, which the conspirators are not spared in *Julius Cæsar*, the Greek Orestes plays, and the *Cinna* of Corneille. Besides, it was then the proper occupation for the revenger biding his time. Men bore in mind the old story of the crafty madness of the elder Brutus, also a revenger; and quite beside the mark for Shakespeare's day is the prevailing notion that the "antic disposition" must have a psychological significance because to our minds it is an artifice lacking in prudence or practical point. Titus Andronicus had been a revenger before Hamlet, and he too was "not essentially in madness but mad in craft."[3] If here Shakespeare saw the unplausibleness of this he ignored it. Unlike Belleforest or the author of the *Fratricide Punished*,

---

[1] Some portion of what I have to say on this subject has already been said in articles, as "Anachronism in Shakespeare Criticism," *Modern Philology* (1910), and others since. I call the reader's attention to this fact because very similar views appear in Professor Schücking's "Primitive Kunstmittel und Moderne Interpretation," *Germanisch-Romanische Monatschrift*, (1912) esp. pp. 330-33. I do not mind Professor Schücking's not being aware of my existence, but I should mind very much seeming myself to be aware, without acknowledging it, of his.

[2] See above, p. 5 *et seq.*

[3] To state it more accurately, Titus both feigned madness, and was mad, like most Elizabethan revengers, Hieronimo, and (perhaps) the original Hamlet. Saturninus speaks of Titus' "feigned ecstasies," IV, iv, 21. Even in *Hamlet* Shakespeare has not handled the situation so carefully as to preclude some question on this head.

we have seen, he offers no explanation. And if he ignored it, pray, how was the Elizabethan audience to be led to perceive it, or turn it into something psychological, in view of the fact that feigned madness had, in the old play—in any revenge play—in Belleforest himself, been presented as the proper and regular thing? *Famam sequere* is the precept, nay, the natural principle; and Shakespeare knows that he is observing it, and that the audience will think he is observing it, unless he makes his contrary intention unmistakably clear.

2

Likewise Hamlet's doubt of the Ghost has been taken for no honest doubt. It is remarkable that scholarly critics continue to do this,[4] although it has long been known that the doctrine that ghosts were masquerading devils was then the enlightened Protestant opinion. If this doctrine had not been taken account of by the dramatist he would simply have been behind the times. As Spalding[5] has shown, it was the doctrine of the Reformers and of such theologians as Hooper and King James I. Says the martyred Bishop, in his *Declaration of the Holy Commaundementes of Allmyghtye God* (1550):

> Those abuse the name of God that seek help of damned spirits, or of such souls as be departed out of this world, as Saul did, . . . or those that by necromancy, or such like enchantments, abuse the name of God to resuscitate dead bodies, or call spirits departed unto the body again; which is nothing else but an illusion and craft of the devil to make men believe lies.[6]

This has to do only with the summoning of the spirits, and it is possible that the Bishop would not have denied that at times ghosts are real enough. But James VI of Scotland, presently to be Shakespeare's sovereign, is quite explicit:

> *Epistemon.* When they appeare vpon that occasion, they are called Wraithes in our language: Amongst the *Gentiles* the diuell vsed that much, to make them beleeue that it was some good spirit that appeared to them then, either to forewarne them of the death of their friend, or else to discouer vnto them the will of the defunct, or what was the way of his slaughter, as it is written in the booke of the histories prodigious: and this way he easily deceiued the *Gentiles*, because they knew not God: and to that same effect is it, that he now appeares in that maner to some ignorant Christians: for hee dares not so illude any that knoweth that, neither can the spirit of the defunct returne to his friend, or yet an Angel vse such formes.—*Dæmonologie*, III, i.[7]

---

[4] Scholars seem often to keep their antiquarian knowledge and their criticism in separate compartments, as students of the Bible do theirs. Mr. E. K. Chambers, whose learning in matters Elizabethan is of course far in excess of anything I can pretend to, nevertheless speaks of Hamlet as "covering his weakness with unreal reasons" (*Warwick* ed.). He surely knows that *per se* the Prince's doubt of the Ghost and his reason for sparing the King were, for a revenge-play, very real.

[5] *Elizabethan Demonology* (1880), pp. 53 ff.

[6] Parker Society ed., p. 326. I regret that I have not the unmodernized text at hand, but the original is very rare.

[7] I quote from *Workes* (1616), p. 125, but this particular treatise first appeared in 1579.

This doctrine is of the soundest, for Henry Smith, "Silver-tongued Smith,"
one of the most eloquent of London preachers in the great Queen's
reign, who died in 1591, speaking of ghosts in his *Pilgrim's Wish*, declares:

> Thus the deuill hath many wayes to deceive; and this is one and a dangerous
> one to draw us from Gods word to visions, and dreames and apparitions, upon
> which many of the doctrines of the Papists are grounded. They had neuer heard of
> Purgatory but for those spirits that walked in the night, and told them that they
> were the soules of such and such, which suffered in fire, till their Masses, and almes,
> and Pilgrimages did ransome them out: so these night-spirits begat Purgatorie, and
> Purgatorye begat Trentals as one Serpent hatcheth another.[8]

And Andrew Willet, in his *Hexapla in Exodum* (1608), p. 81, to the same
effect:

> The divels doe counterfeit the spirits and the soules of the dead; by this means
> the divell more strongly deceiveth, seeing men are readie to heare their parents and
> friends departed.[9]

So Robert Burton, in his *Anatomy* (1621):

> These kind of Devils many times appear to men. . . counterfeiting dead men's
> ghosts, as that of Caligula, which (saith Suetonius) was seen to walk in Lavinia's
> garden, where his body was buried.[10]

This, which is Hamlet's view, had already passed out of the realm of con-
troversy into poetry before him; and the Red Cross Knight cries in answer
to the voice of Fradubio when it comes to him out of the tree:

> What voyce of damned Ghost from Limbo Lake,
> Or guilefull spright wandring in empty aire,
> Both which fraile men do oftentimes mistake,
> Sends to my doubtfull eares these speaches rare?
> *Faerie Queene*, I, ii, 32.   (Cf. II, xi, 39)

And like Hamlet, he too fears that "out of his weakness" the Devil "abuses"
(that is, *deceives*) him. But the skepticism of Sir Thomas Browne in his
Religio (1642), I, Sect. 37, goes farther, and declares the devils no mimics
or counterfeits, but the ghosts themselves, in so far as there are any:

> I believe that these apparitions and ghosts of departed persons are not wander-
> ing souls of men, but the unquiet walks of devils, prompting and suggesting us into
> mischief, blood, and villainy; instilling and stealing into our hearts, that the blessed
> spirits are not at rest in their graves, but wander solicitous of the affairs of the world.[11]

In the same spirit Bacon interprets modern miracles as the "illusions of
spirits,"[12] and Milton does the same with oracles.

---

[8] Hunter's *Illustrations* (1845), ii, p. 211.   But I use the text of *The Sermons*, etc. (1631) pp. 262-63.

[9] Quoted by Halliwell-Phillips, *Memoranda on Hamlet*, p. 9.

[10] Shilleto ed., i, pp. 220-21.

[11] Cited by Coleridge.   Cf. to the same effect the last chapter of Bk. I of the *Pseudodoxia*, where he
interprets most superstitions as the result of the Devil's contriving.

[12] *Advancement of Learning*, I, iv, 9.

The honest doubt or distrust of the supernatural, moreover, is the recognized thing in old stories and plays. However real and indubitable the ghost in Shakespeare may be, he is doubted by the person who had trembled in his presence. There are the several and various cases of Richard III, of Brutus, of Macbeth. And so it is in Tirso's (1571-1648) *Infanzón de Illescas*.[13] Don Pedro, the King, thinks, after the ghost has disappeared, that it was a malicious trick of the Queen's or his brother's. The doubt of the reality of the ghost is the natural psychological reaction of the beholder, once it has vanished. The fear that it may be an evil spirit is equally natural, and also, as here, a means of making a situation, or of retarding the action and prolonging the play. For purposes of story-making this Protestant—supposedly morbid or pusillanimous—misgiving that the spirit may be an evil one, is really ancient and pagan. Stout Odysseus, after Leucothoe had given him the girdle and bid him plunge into the sea, murmurs to himself: "Perhaps this is some god who wishes to destroy me, by ordering me to quit my vessel. I will not do it." And Hamlet's own scruple is none other than that of the elder Hamlet, Orestes (himself surely not weak of heart or of hand), when in Euripides he confesses to Apollo that "there came a dreadful thought into my heart that it was some fiend I had listened to when I seemed to hear thy voice."[14] The simplicity and sincerity of Odysseus and Orestes, surely, is above suspicion, beyond cavil.

If Hamlet, then, were to be represented as deceiving himself when he doubts the Ghost, he should have been given a reason less plausible and natural. If he were meant to be skeptical, he should have been given a reason more original and novel in his day. An hallucination he might have called it, and left the devil out. But if either impression were the one Shakespeare had meant to convey, he could hardly have managed worse. Hamlet doubts the Ghost, but his doubts are so simple and sincere that he can share them with Horatio unabashed, and at once proceed to put them to the proof. He gives the play, and upon the blenching of the King his doubts are forever settled. "I'll take the Ghost's word," he cries, "for a thousand pound." But if the play had been a pretext or subterfuge, would he not have forgotten the pretended purpose of it—noted the King's guilt but not remembered the word of the Ghost? Or if he had been the incorrigible skeptic that since Coleridge and Schlegel's day he has been thought to be, would he not have doubted still? Leontes

---

[13] I, iv.—On this subject see my article on Ghosts in Shakespeare, *M. L. P.*, xxii, 217-18.

[14] *Orestes*, ll. 1668-69; and also Orestes in the *Electra*, l. 979: "Surely it was a fiend in the likeness of the god that commanded this." The word in both cases is *alastor*. Again, in the *Iphigeneia in Tauris*, Orestes complains that "Phoebus deceived us by his prophecies." In the first two instances the parallel is clear—it is the revenger of his father's death, doubting, momentarily, the genuineness of the mandate of revenge which he has received from the other world. For evidence of the influence of Euripides on the old *Hamlet*, see the *Appendix*.

continues to doubt Hermione's innocence after the oracle is delivered
which he had sought. But Hamlet's doubt is as simple as old Hieronimo's.
Belimperia's letter he thinks a trap; but having learnt the truth through
the intercepted letter of Pedringano, he, like Hamlet, seeks no further,
doubts no more. In the plot of both plays doubt seems to perform an
identical function. In Hamlet's case, moreover, it is prepared for, not
dragged in. The pretext, if such it be, occurs long before he has need of
it, or can have a "forefeeling"[15] of such need, the Ghost having as yet
not unsealed his lips:

> Be thou a spirit of health or *goblin damned*. .

Nor is that a sign that his wit is diseased if we remember Brutus' question as he faces Cæsar's ghost:

> Art thou some god, some angel, or some devil?

Indeed, there are several passages, as Spalding has shown,[16] which imply
that the night on the platform both Hamlet and Horatio were fully aware
that a ghost was a dubious and dangerous thing.

It is of course to be admitted that Hamlet otherwise does not act as
if he doubted—does not in any way change his attitude to the King. In
the nunnery scene he tells Ophelia that those who are married—*all but
one*—shall live; and in the play scene he is insulting and menacing from
the start. But that is Shakespeare's way. Leontes, after all, does not
doubt Hermione, Posthumus does not doubt Imogen, Othello does not
doubt Desdemona after the temptation scene. Doubt means suspension of
belief, or wavering betwixt belief and disbelief. These heroes do not waver
—do not simply fail to believe their wives true, but positively believe them
false. Shakespeare has no technique, we have noted,[17] for presenting hesitation or irresolution, deliberation or debate; and of doubt may be said
the same. His characters are on the one side or the other—they do not
tarry in the twilight—amid the debatable lands—in between. Not intellect

---

[15] I allude to Professor Bradley's subtle and much-praised device for explaining something quite different,—why Hamlet should decide upon madness (his "safety-valve," and his first evasion) at once, and
not—for the first time—after he had found his courage ebbing. Hamlet had a "forefeeling" of his need.
(*Op. cit.*, pp. 120-21). Of this Shakespeare gives no hint, and surely nothing could be further removed from
the spirit of his or any dramatic art. A play is not a puzzle. Besides, this notion interferes with Mr. Bradley's own conception of Hamlet as a strong man. See my article, *Kittredge Anniversary Papers*, p. 269.

[16] Pp. 55-59. Cf. in particular the echo of James VI's words. Horatio cries:
> What if it tempt you toward the flood, my lord,
> Or to the dreadful summit of the cliff,
> Etc.

Dæmonologie (III, ii):
> It is to obtaine one of two things thereby, if he [the Devil] may: The one is the tinsell of their life,
> by inducing them to such perillous places, at such time as he either followes or possesses them, which may
> procure the same, and such like, so farre as God will permit him, by tormenting them to weaken their
> bodie, and cast them into incurable diseases.

[17] See above, p. 7, note 19.

is the centre of their being but emotion and imagination. If they doubt, it is, as with Hamlet, only to make assurance doubly sure. Hamlet's doubt of the King's guilt, then, is not searching and thorough-going, but it is not therefore to be considered specious or unreal. If he fails to take his doubt to heart we are not therefore to think his doubt a pretext. It is not so much he who fails to take his doubt to heart as it is his maker. Though natural enough in the character, his doubt mainly serves as a *retardierendes Moment* in the story; and it is not by us to be taken psychologically—least of all for such a reason as that it was not taken psychologically by Shakespeare himself.

3

The greatest hoax, however, that Hamlet is supposed to have played on himself is when he spares the King at prayer. He shrinks from the deed, but he deceives his conscience by the promise of a more complete and horrible vengeance when the King is about an act that has no relish of salvation in it. With the numerous remoter explanations offered we shall not concern ourselves, whether it be a lack of will power, his unwillingness to kill a defenceless man, or an aversion to killing in general. What interests us is whether in this matter he deceives himself at all.

Here again the reason actually given is, for a revenge play, right and proper. It is consistent, in the first place, with the rest of the play. In Shakespeare's final version Hamlet retains not merely this but many other bloody Kydian sentiments and qualities. "Would I had met my dearest foe in Heaven, Horatio," Hamlet exclaims as he thinks of his mother's wedding, "or ever I had seen that day." "Now could I drink hot blood," he cries before he goes to his mother's bedchamber, just before he meets the King. And on his trip to England he does not hesitate to send Rosencrantz and Guildenstern to their death, as he puts it, "not shriving-time allowed." The reason he gives himself for postponing vengeance, moreover, tallies completely with the Ghost's own tale of his bitter lot, and thereby the audience is prepared to accept his reason. Hamlet says:

> He took my father grossly and full of bread,
> With all his crimes broad blown, as flush as May;
> And how his audit stands who knows save Heaven?
> But in our circumstance and course of thought
> 'Tis heavy with him. And am I then reveng'd
> To take him in the purging of his soul,
> When he is fit and season'd for his passage?

And his father had said before that:

> Cut off even in the blossoms of my sin,
> Unhousel'd, disappointed, unanel'd,
> No reckoning made, but sent to my account
> With all my imperfections on my head,
> O, horrible! O, horrible! most horrible!

In the second place, any one who is familiar with revenge tragedy, whether that of the ancients or of the Renaissance, is aware that the principle which prevails in it is an eye for an eye, a tooth for a tooth; and the blow in return may be greater but not less than the injury. Even with the selfsame axe which felled Agamemnon the son must needs smite the murderess and her paramour. "The justice of it pleases." And the answer to Hamlet's question is that neither in classical nor in Renaissance tragedy would he seem to be revenged if he took the King in the purging of his soul.

Indeed, the expression of a longing to kill both body and soul, which in this case Samuel Johnson thought too horrible to be read or uttered, is far from rare in Elizabethan drama and literature. Two perfect parallels are found in early prose. There is that in the *Brief Discourse of the Spanish State, with a Dialogue annexed, entitled Philobasilis* (1590), p. 24:

> One of these monsters meeting his enemie unarmed, threatened to kill him if he denied not God, his power, and essential properties, viz. his mercy, suffrance, etc., the which when the other, desiring life, pronounced with great horror, kneeling upon his knees; the hero cried out, *nowe will I kill thy body and soule*, and at that instant thrust him through with his rapier.[18]

And there is that in Nash's *Jack Wilton* (1594):

> [Cutwolf has led his enemy on, in the hope of saving himself, to utter abominable blasphemies and devote his soul to the devil.] "These fearefull ceremonies brought to an end, I bad him ope his mouth and gape wide. He did so (as what wil not slaues do for feare?); therewith made I no more ado, but shot him full into the throat with my pistoll; no more spake he after; so did I shoot him that he might neuer speak after, or repent him."[19]

Quite so, in the anonymous *Alphonsus Emperor of Germany* (published 1654) Alexander induces his victim to renounce the joys of heaven as the price of his life, and in that moment takes his life as well:

> *Alphonsus.* Alphonsus doth renounce the joyes of Heaven,
> The sight of Angells and his Saviours blood,
> And gives his soul unto the Devills power.
> *Alexander.* Thus will I make delivery of the Deed,
> Die and be damn'd, now am I satisfied.
> V, i.

Heywood in his *Gynaikeion, or Nine Bookes of Various History Concerninge Women* (1624), tells a similar story of "a gentleman of Mediolanum," "that hauing his enemie at his mercie, held his steeletto to his heart, and swore that unlesse he would instantly abiure his faith, and renounce his Sauiour, had he a thou-

[18] Cited by Reed, Furness, i, p. 283.

[19] McKerrow, ii, p. 326. In his notes Mr. McKerrow refers also to Browne's *Religio Medici*, the anonymous notes, ed. Sayle, i, p. 1, where the same story is told. The passages from Nash and the *Alphonsus* are cited by Creizenach.

sand liues he would instantly (with as many wounds) despoile him of all; which the other for feare assenting to, and he, hauing made him iterate ouer and ouer his un-christianlike blasphemies, in the middle of his horrible abiuration stabd him to the heart, uttering these words, See, I am reueng'd of thy soule and bodie at once; for as thy bodie is desperate of life, so is thy soule of mercie." (P. 400)[20]

So in John Ford's *'Tis Pity She's a Whore* (1627) V, iv, the servant suggests to the infuriated Soranzo, whose wife has been guilty of incest with her brother: "Let my hot hare [her brother] have law[21] ere he be hunted to his death, that, if it be possible, he post to hell in the very act of his damnation."[22]

Without such ingenious contrivances to make it effective, moreover, there is still more frequently expressed the simple and emphatic wish to send your victim's soul to hell. It is thus that Belimperia admonishes her tardy father-in-law.

> For heere I sweare, in sight of heauen and earth,
> Shouldst thou neglect the loue thou shouldst retaine,
> And giue it ouer, and deuise no more,
> Myselfe should send their hatefull soules to hell,
> That wrought his downfall with extreamest death.
> *Spanish Tragedy*, IV, i, 25-30.

In the same spirit Hieronimo invokes further vengeance on these murderers the moment that he has killed them.

> Upon whose soules may heauens be yet auenged
> With greater far than these afflictions.
> IV, iv, 173-74.

And at the very end of the play the Ghost of Andrea in fifteen specific lines allots to each of them his own particular portion of damnation and everlasting pain. Indeed, there is every evidence that to Kyd's account is to be reckoned this sentiment of Hamlet's which we are now considering.

It is a sentiment frequently met with on the lips of heroes of that type of Senecan tragedy to which the *Spanish Tragedy* and *Hamlet* belong. Frequently it takes the form of embittering the victim's last moments by taunting him with thoughts of the hell to which he is hastening. So it is in *Antonio's Revenge* (1599) V, ii, 100-104; the *First Part of Jeronimo* (1602?) I, iii, 79-80; Tourneur's *Revenger's Tragedy* (1607) III, iv; and Webster's *White Devil* (1612) V, i, pp. 117-118 (1857, vol. ii). In Italian tragedy of the sixteenth century, it would seem, the Senecan *atrocitas* took a form still nearer to that in *Hamlet*. Merope, at least, in the tragedy of that name by Pomponio Torelli (1589), finding the supposed murderer

---

[20] Referred to by McKerrow, *ut supra*.

[21] A hunting term, meaning a head start.

[22] This is parallel to Hamlet at another point, III, iii, 90:
> When he is drunk asleep, or in his rage,
> Or in the incestuous pleasure of his bed.

of her son asleep, will not kill him so. He would die "too happy"; but she would harm, if she could, both body and soul ("insieme il corpo e l'alma").[23] And she rouses him for the same reasons as Beaumont and Fletcher's Evadne when she rouses her King out of his sleep.

> Yet I must not
> Thus tamely do it, as he sleeps; that were
> To rock him to another world, etc.
>
> *Maid's Tragedy* (1609), V, ii.

But some of these may seem to us rather sorry ladies and gentlemen, of whom better were not to be expected, though as a matter of fact they have not so much blood on their heads as the high-souled Prince. To reassure us, there is, in a play in which Shakespeare himself had a hand, the *Second Part of Henry VI* (1591-2), Iden, the philosophizing and moralizing squire of Kent, who says, as he kills the rebel Cade:

> And as I thrust thy body in with my sword,
> So wish I, I might thrust thy soul to hell.
>
> IV, x, 84-85.

And in Belleforest's novel, the hero is almost as vindictive as our Senecan Hamlet:

> "Et pour ce va," he cries as he fells him with his hand, "et estant aux enfers, ne faux de compter à ton frere, que tu occis meschamment, que c'est son fils qui te fait faire ce message a fin que soulagé par ceste memoire, son ombre s'appaise parmy les esprits bien heureux."—(*Lyon*, 1576) p. 259.

Amleth keeps the body to show to the Danes that they may wreak vengeance on it,—

> affin que ce soit vous qui punissez le tronc, et charoigne morte, puis que vivãt il n'est peu tomber en voz mains, pour en faire entiere la punition et vengeance et rassasier vostre colere, sur les oz de celuy, etc.—*Ib*. p. 271.

So he bids them burn the body and scatter the ashes, putting "the sparks of pity" far from them,

> affin que ny la cruche d'argent, ou cristal, ny un sacré tombeau soient le repos des reliques, et ossements d'un homme si detestable.

4

All this is literary and dramatic evidence. Before quitting it, we might well pause and consider a moment whether, not merely for this ferocity but for revenge of any sort as a duty, evidence can be drawn from Elizabethan life. Some few critics, particularly the German, have insisted that in the England of Shakespeare's time the *jus talionis* was still in force. One may be permitted to doubt if it was in force so fully as it is in certain regions of the United States today, where family and clan feuds still per-

---

[23] Ed. Verona (1723), pp. 381-82.

sist, and where, in case of adultery, is openly pleaded "the unwritten law." From Reeves, Stephen, Wordsworth, and Coke himself it would appear that, whether adultery or murder be the cause, it could not be pleaded before English courts—the right of blood-feud was done away with in Anglo-Saxon times, if indeed it ever existed[24]—nor does the record of events in Elizabethan England indicate that the vendetta was then a custom. "The Italian vendetta," says Sir Walter Raleigh, "of which so many terrible pictures are to be found in the dramatists, came into English literature rather than into English life."[25] But even so, it came early, and for the most part not through direct contact with Italy but through the pages of Seneca. Just as without the motive of revenge there would have been no Senecan tragedy, so there would have been no *Gorboduc*, no *Hamlet*, *Titus Andronicus*, or *Richard III*. Even the morals of marital retaliation, as in *Othello*, are stage morals; and so they are (though in less measure) in the plays which deal with the "point of honor" in Spain. This the great Lope several times admits. "In the Preface to the twentieth volume of his Theatre, he confesses, with reference to his own 'Wise Vengeance,' that its title is absurd, because all revenge is unwise and unlawful."[26] Shakespeare could have said as much. And yet, though he thus expresses himself against revenge, "it seems," as Ticknor observes, "as if one half of Lope's plays go to justify it." And almost the same might be said of the pious Calderon. In fact, it is only in the present day that Spanish drama has dared to throw over the convention as regards the jealous husband, and even in English drama and story the revenge convention lasted into the eighteenth century. Drama, says M. Maeterlinck (though a bit exaggerating), "est encore plus lent que tous les autres arts à suivre les évolutions de la conscience humaine."

The error in question is that of which the critic of criticism must ever complain—the confounding of life and literature, of history and art. But a similar error, with more serious consequences, is committed by those critics who take the opposite point of view, and recognizing that the vendetta was not established in Elizabethan England, and that Shakespeare in real life could not have countenanced it, hold that Hamlet has scruples against the deed, or that nothing less than justice will content him. To one who sticks to the text and reads it, not as a piece of poetry and philosophy, but as a play, it is evident that Hamlet, like every other Elizabethan revenger, seeks revenge on the murderer and nothing more. It is not only his duty but his desire; and like Sophocles' Orestes he "must not"—would not—"spare him any bitterness of death."[27]

[24] Pollock and Maitland (1898), i, pp. 450-51.

[25] *Shakespeare's England*, i, p. 30.

[26] Ticknor, *Spanish Literature* (1863), ii, p. 263. But for contemporary Spanish custom see Menendez y Pelayo, *Calderon y su teatro*, pp. 279-80.

[27] L. 1504.

To argue one's way out of that is but to do what Professor Wilamowitz-Moellendorff has done to the Orestes of Æschylus. It may well be that in Æschylus' time a belief in a family nemesis or curse, or in the *devoir* of the vendetta, or of blind obedience to the god such as was Orestes' to Apollo, was no longer cherished by the noblest of the Greeks. But that is neither here nor there when we are reading the Æschylean trilogy. If Orestes be under no obligation to obey the god and kill his father's murderers (though that he is, all the good characters, the chorus, and not only Apollo but Athena, the goddess of wisdom herself, declare) we must come to the conclusion that Æschylus did not pen a drama for thousands of his simple fellow-citizens, but, flying in the face of all the principles of dramatic art as he did it, contrived riddles for the wise and few. But Æschylus is like Shakespeare—even in the fate that has since befallen him.

5

Hamlet gives a reason, then, such as was to be expected, not of a gentleman in London or Stratford, but of a character in a revenge tragedy, or in almost any tragedy, of his time. He gives a reason that is in keeping with other atrocious sentiments and deeds of his in this very play. Indeed, he gives a reason which must already have been offered by the early Hamlet before him,[28] and which, as I take it, no scholar can successfully maintain to have been given otherwise than in perfect good faith. Could, then, the Elizabethan audience, for whom alone the play was written, have understood that the reason presented in all good faith in the old play was now, when retained in the new version, but a shift or subterfuge?[29] Even in a new story a subterfuge must be clearly indicated, but it is doubly necessary that it should be in the case of an already familiar story, and a striking incident in it.

But what if the audience were expecting from the dramatist something new and original? Even then there are difficulties. Manifestly Hamlet does not deceive himself unless Shakespeare intended him to deceive himself. Manifestly Hamlet does not deceive himself except as Shakespeare conveys that thought. There is no self-deception (just as there is no character of Hamlet) except as it is conveyed to the audience by means of words and the conventions of dramatic art. Many readers there are, to be sure, who fail to remember this. Bound by the dramatist's potent spell,

---

[28] Not only is it the reason furnished in the *Fratricide Punished*, but also, with some modification, that in the same situation in *Antonio's Revenge* (1599), III, i, 137, cited above, p. 15 note 4. Antonio will not kill him till, like Titus Andronicus, he has served up to him a Thyestean banquet. Like Hamlet he keeps his promise.

[29] Cf. the notion of Stahr that Cleopatra in concealing her treasure was only acting a part and trying to make Caesar and his men think she intended to live, and in lying and getting caught at it was really catching them. Such subtlety is made doubly impossible by the spectators' knowledge of Plutarch's story. Cf. MacCallum, *Shakespeare's Roman Plays* (1910), p. 433.

they forget that fiction is not truth, drama not biography, Hamlet or Othello not flesh and blood and bone. Hence they are capable of finding a character self-deceptive, even drunk[30] or crazy, whether his creator intended him to be so or not. They are wise above that which is written. They know Hamlet or Othello better than their dearest friends, they say, and the teller of the story, like his purpose in telling it, is nothing to them. All that counts is the story, and what they can make of it; and they discover in it what to the teller himself was never known. They even discover in it what was directly contrary to his intention, and tell the story over again for themselves. To those who persist in this sort of mental confusion, taking upon themselves the mystery of things and writing the private history of beings who are not and cannot be,—who are shadows, wraiths, nothing whatever but the figments of a poet's brain,—the considerations which we are now urging can, of course, have no point or meaning.

6

There are several ways in which self-deception can be made apparent on the stage, none of which is here employed. Chief of these is that the reason given should itself be far-fetched, transparently thin and specious. In the novel it may be less so, but on the stage a subterfuge must fairly look like one. There is no mistaking Falstaff's, Bob Acres', or Hjalmar Ekdal's. But, just as in real life, if it be a natural or usual reason we do not wink or look askance. Hamlet's reason is natural, we have seen, and consistent; and people nowadays think it not such simply because they do not enter into the spirit of Elizabethan drama. People began to complain of it only far along into the eighteenth century,—the author of *Some Remarks* in 1736, "A Well-wisher and Admirer" in a letter to Garrick in 1742,[31] Johnson in 1765, Tom Davies in 1785.[32] It was too horrible, said one and all. They had been alienated, by now, from the Senecan tradition—

Verbannet ist der Sitten falsche Strenge—

the humane and sentimental spirit reigned. They complained of his reason, but they did not presume to doubt it. Then, by a trick of the human

---

[30] For an example of this, in a very sensible book, see Professor Wendell's *William Shakespeare* (1894), p. 171. This whole matter of ignoring the author's intention, and of confounding his conceptions with the substantive realities of life I have repeatedly discussed before, especially in my articles on *Shylock* (1910) and *Falstaff* (1914) and my monograph on *Othello* (1915).

[31] From Dublin, *Private Correspondence of David Garrick* (1831), i, p. 14.

[32] III, p. 104: "The first actor who rejected this horrid soliloquy was Mr. Garrick." From the letter cited above it appears that in 1742 Garrick had not rejected it. "Well-wisher" beseeches him to omit it, as "a terrible blot and stain to a character, that, were it not for that, would be complete." But as yet no one went behind the returns. Voltaire (*v. ante*) in 1761 took the reality of the motive for granted. (*Œuvres*, xxiv, p. 198). And the author of *Miscellaneous Observations on Hamlet*, 1752, in commenting on Hamlet's words "I his sole son, do this same Villain send To Heaven," makes this observation and no more: "Hamlet means by it that he was his *only* son, and consequently ought to be his chief avenger, instead of doing an Act of Kindness to his Assassin" (p. 39).

brain which has, hundreds of times, repeated itself in the history of literature (as indeed in the history of religion too) what they did not like they instinctively put from them and explained away.   So, by his words in 1784, Richardson, the Glasgow professor, became the voice of his age: "The sentiments that Hamlet expresses when he finds Claudius at prayer, are not, I will venture to affirm, his real ones."[33]

Another way of securing the effect of self-deception is by means of repetition.   As I have remarked elsewhere, if here the man were really meant to flinch, he would be made to do so once more.   In all times, and particularly in early times, in order to make a point dramatists have found it necessary to drive it home; and there would be a special necessity for this in the case of so difficult a matter as self-deception in tragedy.   There is such a necessity even in matters less difficult.   If Brutus is an impractical idealist, he must thwart Cassius's worldly prudence, not only in the matter of the oath but also in the matter of letting Antony speak to the People and in the strategy at Philippi.   If Coriolanus is proud and contemptuous, he must be made not once but twice to undertake to win the favor of the People and break down in the doing of it.   But Hamlet, flinching, if you will, when the King is delivered into his hands at prayer, at his next opportunity to kill a man who, apparently, is the King, *kills* him; and there is only one thing for an audience to think of that.   In the very next scene he has caught the King, as he thinks, "about an act that has no relish of salvation in it," and is as good as his word.   It is not the King—but what, then, is the King about when the Prince catches him in the end?   Trafficking in death and treachery, poisoning foils and bowls.   It has paid to wait.   "This physic doth but prolong thy sickly days," Hamlet had confidently said as he left his uncle on his knees.   It was not the speech, as the event proves, of one who fails in deeds and takes refuge in words.

Nay, but there again he is deceiving himself, the critics protest.   He doesn't really believe it is the King, they say despite the plain intention of the text;[34] or, he is striking out frantically because of his failure before; or, he can act on the spur of the moment, as he cannot in resolute fulfilment of a duty; or, he can stab a man through the arras, but not eye to eye, not face to face.   One wonders whether these writers ever stop to consider how a stage play is made, or how audiences, or even readers, make shift to comprehend it.   There is a recognized method and medium of expres-

---

[33] *Essays on Shakespeare's Characters* (1798), p. 131. See above, p. 8, note 22.

[34] "Is it the King?"—"I took thee for thy better." And the intention being so plain, even the cleverest critics, before the days of Romanticism, refrained from tampering with it; as Voltaire (*Œuvres*, 24, p. 198), and the author of *Some Remarks* (1736): "Our Hero had not put him to Death, had he not thought it to have been the Usurper hid behind the Arras (pp. 43-44). Even Davies, in 1784 (*Miscellanies*, Ed. 1785, iii, pp. 104-5) in criticising Voltaire's carelessness, whom he seems to misunderstand, makes the same observation as he: "Had he read the play . . . . he would have known that Hamlet imagined that the person he had killed was the King himself." Throughout his long commentary Davies nowhere suggests the likelihood of self-deception or unconscious fiction.

sion, a language of the drama, in short,—"simple and sensuous," and certainly sensible,—which one must speak and the other understand. And if it be to me a language not wholly strange and foreign, there is only one possible way (without explicit comment to guide us) whereby Hamlet can, as here, be represented as shrinking from the deed and at the same time deceiving himself,—and that is by acting as he did before. If now he had hesitated; if now again he had deferred the hour of reckoning and prolonged the King's sickly days; or if once afterwards he had been given an opportunity and failed to take advantage of it: then it would have been clear that his hesitation before had been a fault, and the reason he gave a swindle. Since he does not hesitate, but strikes instantly, on the spur of the moment, it is clear that the reason for delay he had given was an honest reason, and that he now stoutly keeps his word.

Still another, a third way, of presenting self-deception, is that just now suggested—explicit comment. This may be by the character himself, or by the others on the stage. It is strange indeed that in this, Shakespeare's most subtle and difficult play (though not so subtle and difficult as criticism has made it) there should have been, as we have seen, no comment on the tragic fault, if such there be. Shakespeare's other chief characters, even those who, like Lear, would in real life have known themselves but slenderly, know their weaknesses very well; but Hamlet "does not know" nor does any of his friends. And as for the self-deception, it is Shakespeare's wont to make that perfectly clear. There may be the comment of another, as when Othello cries "Not a jot, not a jot!" in rejoinder to Iago's remark, "I see this hath a little dash'd your spirits." "I' faith I fear it has," he insists, with hypocritical regret and icy candor. But when there are no witnesses the character must needs bear witness against himself. There is in *Othello* another instance of this, when Iago for the moment dallies with the notion that he cannot be called a villain; and one in this very play when Hamlet falls a' cursing like a very drab and catches himself at it.[35] It is strange that Shakespeare thought good plainly to label this case of self-deception, and yet let the presumably

---

[35] In the soliloquy "O What a Rogue," Act II, ii, 610 ff.—This sort of self-deception is not complete, for in the end the deceiver knows that he deceives himself. But no other sort is possible in soliloquy, at least in Elizabethan tragedy. The obvious irony of double-tongued soliloquies, such as Falstaff's, is only an apparent exception. (See my "Falstaff," *Mod. Phil.*, xii, pp. 233-34.) If I may be permitted to quote from my article "*Anachronism in Shakespeare Criticism*," (*ib.*, April, 1910, pp. 561-62): "Whatever a character says in soliloquy concerning his motives is for the information of the audience and is necessarily true. Iago is a liar no doubt, but it is to confound fact with fiction and knock the props from under Shakespeare's dramatic framework to hold that Iago's soliloquies are lies—that he lies to the audience, lies to himself. His word concerning his motives, like the theological reason Hamlet renders himself for sparing the King at prayer, must be taken at its face value. There is no chance of the audience discounting it, for they have no other clue." And that applies to the suggestion which Professor Bradley entertains as to Prince Hal's deceiving himself in his first soliloquy (*Oxford Lectures*, 1914, p. 254). I refer to the words: "I know you all and will awhile uphold the unyok'd humour of your idleness," etc. If a case of self-deception, how was the audience to discover that it is? Instead of being unpleasant and unnatural to them, as it is to us, this soliloquy preserved in their eyes the reputation of a famous English King.

momentous cases like the resolve on the play as the thing, the sparing of the King at prayer, and the summoning up of his energies on his departure for England, go unmarked. It is strange that he should let Hamlet trip himself up when he unpacks his heart with words, and yet never let him detect himself—suspect himself—in culpable evasion, or once doubt he should do the deed when the occasion called. That Shakespeare should do thus, and yet conceive of Hamlet as deceiving himself thus, is too strange a thing to be.

Nothing vexes a popular dramatist more than to be misunderstood—for him there is not the consolation in store that there is for poet or prophet —but according to the critics Shakespeare in *Hamlet* must have courted it. He would make, for once, not a play for the stage but a puzzle and riddle for the ages! And as chance would have it—for what is art, to be sure, but a matter of chance?—it turned out to be the first of stage plays in England, and for two hundred years no one realized that there was a riddle at all! But we know in our souls that the right element of art is not chance and the unexpected; not obscurity or confusion. Even the most esoteric art must find ready access to the minds and hearts of men, and drama must find it swiftly and surely. Elsewhere, as we have seen; Shakespeare has not thought it beneath his dignity to furnish comment on the tragic fault, if there be one, or on the self-deception. Now Shakespeare is far less restricted in his appeal, less exacting in his demands upon the attention and understanding—more popular, in short—than Ibsen. But with what elaborate repetition and variation of situation, with what cunning contrast of character with character and of character with circumstance, and with what plenitude of comment, Ibsen presents to us the self-righteous self-deception of Helmer in the *Doll's House* or the sentimental self-deception of Hjalmar in the *Wild Duck!* In the *Doll's House* comment is provided through Nora; in the *Wild Duck* through Relling and the comically—pathetically—mistaken Gina, Gregers, and Hedvig. Thus upon the self-deception in the two plays many rays of light converge; but in *Hamlet* it is otherwise.

One thing at least the dramatist might have done in case he shrank from having others perceive Hamlet's propensity or from having him perceive the mental process on the occasion himself. If really he beguiled himself when he spared the King, why on a later occasion, particularly in his last soliloquy, before setting out for England, does he not clearly recognize it? Why is he, the most reflective and analytic character in Shakespeare, never permitted to bring against himself any definite charge, whether of self-deception or of conscious dereliction of duty?

7

There is a passage, however, preliminary to Hamlet's sparing the King, which bids us pause. At the end of the play-scene, just before he answers the call to his mother, Hamlet speaks the soliloquy, "'Tis now the very witching time of night," in which he pronounces himself ready to drink hot blood,

> And do such bitter business as the day
> Would quake to look on.

But when next he appears and finds the King, he stays his hand. This may seem to be real evidence of irresolution, not the fanciful or arbitrary notion of a reader. These words, moreover, about churchyards yawning, hell breathing out, and our hero drinking hot blood, do not appear in Quarto 1. Did Shakespeare intend them, then, to contrast Hamlet's big intentions with his pitiful performance?

I will not undertake to show that the sentiments are more in the vein of Kyd and Marston[36] than of Shakespeare; but even if they be Shakespeare's addition, he took care to direct the current of feeling in them wholly toward the Queen, whom Hamlet had just been bid come and see.

> Soft: now to my Mother.
> O heart, lose not thy nature! Let not ever
> The soul of Nero enter this firm bosom;
> Let me be cruel, not unnatural.
> I will speak daggers to her but use none.

Though it is probable that in the words previous to these he was thinking of revenge and his uncle, he has not a word here to say either of him or of revenge.[37] That, however, is not the important thing, but whether this soliloquy is meant to contrast with Hamlet's words when next he appears. On the contrary, it is in accord. His thought keeps its course. He spares the King only out of the hardness of his heart—in the rigor of his revenge—and not because he could not stab a man who was praying or who had not his sword then in hand. It would be another thing if before this he had shown relentings or indifference. And still more is the soliloquy in accord with Hamlet's deeds. Out flies his weapon on the instant, just as it does in the following scene, in the bedchamber:

> Now might I do it pat, now he is praying.
> And now I'll do't—And so he goes to heaven;
> And so am I reveng'd.

The trouble is that modern readers look for the minor likenesses and contrasts;[38] but if we are true to Shakespeare and to Elizabethan art we shall

---

[36] They are parallel to Antonio's words just before he kills Julio, *A.R.*, III, i, 184:

> Now barks the wolf against the full-cheek'd moon,
> . . . .
> Now gapes the graves and through their yawns let loose
> Imprison'd spirits to revisit earth.

[37] If Shakespeare had meant to contrast Hamlet's big words with his small performance he should have had his hero comport himself more as in the brutal German version. There (II, ix) he vows vengeance on the King and goes straightway to find him. But finding him, he blenches. If this be nearer the original, Shakespeare, in turn, has obscured the contrast, and again rescued the character.

[38] It has even been argued that Hamlet shows his insincerity in going, after his words about drinking hot blood, to see his Mother, not to seek out the King. He goes, of course, because he is sent for and had already promised to go. His thoughts are on his Mother, we have seen, in this very speech.

dwell on the bigger, more obvious ones. Despite the minor contrasts and differences, the three situations hold like the stones of an arch together, —the words about the bitter business, the sparing of the King for a more fearful end, when he shall be about an act that hath no relish of salvation in it, and the killing of him (as Hamlet thinks) when in the bedchamber he has at last caught him about it, on the spot. One centripetal force holds all three—the identity of Hamlet's revengeful spirit. The last two situations, indeed, are to each other as question and answer, promise and promise-keeping. If we doubted him at the beginning, we wholly believe in him here at the end.

The contrast found by Professor Bradley, along with the host of literary critics before him, is that between actions deliberate and impulsive. "The chance comes so suddenly that he has no time to scan it."[39] Such a *nuance* as that, any playwright knows, would, in the big masses of light and shadow flung upon the stage, be wholly lost and swallowed up. What is far more to the point than such niggling refinements as these is Professor Bradley's remarks about the sympathies of the audience. They would be on the Prince's side, as he says, when he spares a man at prayer and kills a spy.[40] That being the case, the attention of the audience would be drawn not to minor inconsistencies, which are discoverable, but to the prevailing consistency of the hero's conduct, which is apparent. And what the audience, not what critics, would think and feel, is, I must weary the reader with repeating, alone what Shakespeare had in mind and at heart.

[39] P. 137. This distinction has been accepted for more than a century, but even if it were intended I doubt its validity as a bit of psychology. The meeting with the King had been as unexpected as with the man behind the arras. Why did he not act *then?* The better psychology, as it seems to me, is, that the healthy man of action who had just lost a chance would snatch the next impetuously. He would not wait a moment, and so much the less if he thinks it is the King. This psychology, at any rate, has the advantage of being simpler, as well as more definitely related to the situation of a man who is keeping the promise he had made to himself.

[40] Pp. 136, 137. This Mr. Bradley calls a "minor consideration"; I consider it an mportant one. And the killing of the man behind the arras, Mr. Bradley thinks intended to "stand in sharp contrast with the sparing of his enemy." I think it is in harmony,—the authentication of the motive Hamlet alleges, the deed to match his word.

CHAPTER V
THE END OF THE PLAY
1

The conclusion of a play is one of the surest indexes to your dramatist's thought. It is so with the Greeks, for with them there is always the final choral comment; it is so with Ibsen, for in the end he has stripped the soul of the hero or heroine bare; it is equally so with the Elizabethans. The chorus here, we have already seen, is Fortinbras. But what is Hamlet himself concerned for at the last, after his work is done? Mainly for his "wounded name."

> Report me and my cause aright
> To the unsatisfied!

Nothing in the words or the situation will justify any interpretation except that Hamlet is anxious to have the world know why he had killed his uncle the King. For his name suffers not at all because of his procrastination; no one knows of the murder of his father, still less of his spirit's mandate. Hamlet's interest is in his name being cleared, his reputation being righted, and after that in the news from England, and in the succession to the throne. Not a thought has he for any fault or defect[1] such as Othello reveals in his last words for his. Not a thought, either, for his triumph over it. "Done after all," is what he should say to himself if he were the crippled, aspiring but despairing, spirit the critics have taken him to be. Dramatic art—human nature itself—would demand no less. If the tragedy be, as the critics maintain, internal, here, if nowhere else, that fact must come to light. The audience must see it, if the other characters do not. But Hamlet's only interests now are in things external—his name, the news, his father's crown. "The rest is *silence*," the critics pick up his words to answer; and they put a world of meaning into the phrase that could never have been intended, because it could never have been understood. The words simply mean:—I am a dead man, the rest must go untold.

What goes untold Horatio is to tell. (In Shakespeare what ever goes untold, and to him is of moment? His words—of all men's—were neither faint nor few.) Horatio has been commissioned to give the "complete official report." But this is to come, he says, after the play is over, and that implies that it would be only what the audience already know. Meantime he gives a summary of it, the headlines, so to speak, without,

---

[1] Mr. Stopford Brooke, for instance (*Ten More Plays of Shakespeare*, N. Y., 1913, p. 137), declares that he has. What I am insisting on, however, is not that the best critics generally lend their authority to such an interpretation, but that here, if anywhere, such sentiments would, if the critics otherwise are right, necessarily appear. And they do not appear.

however, hinting at any failure or shortcoming in the hero.   To him, the Prince's friend, the tragedy is not by any means what we are inclined to take it for—simply the tragedy of Hamlet's soul.   "So shall you hear," he cries to the wondering Danes at the end:

> Of carnal, bloody, and unnatural acts,
> Of accidental judgments, casual slaughters,
> Of deaths put on by cunning and forc'd cause,
> And, in this upshot, purposes mistook
> Fallen on the inventors' heads.

A tragedy, that is to say (though so much else besides that) of intrigue, fate, and blood.   And exactly such it was taken to be in the earliest extended criticism, to which we have already alluded, that in James Drake's *Antient and Modern Stages Survey'd* (1699):

> Nothing in Antiquity can rival this plot for the admirable distribution of Poetick Justice.   The Criminals are not only brought to execution, but they are taken in their own Toyls, their own Stratagems recoyl upon 'em, and they are involved themselves in that mischief and ruine, which they had projected for *Hamlet*.   *Polonius* by playing the Spy meets a Fate, which was neither expected by nor intended for him.   *Guildenstern* and *Rosencrans*, the Kings Decoys, are counter-plotted, and sent to meet that fate, to which they were trepanning the Prince.   The Tyrant himself falls by his own plot, and by the hand of the Son of that Brother, whom he had Murther'd.   *Laertes* suffers by his own Treachery, and dies by a Weapon of his own preparing.   Thus every one's crime naturally produces his Punishment, and every one (the Tyrant excepted) commences a Wretch almost as soon as a Villain.[2]

To something of the same effect is the opinion of the author of *Some Remarks* (1736) as he touches on poetic justice in the death of Laertes and the Queen:

> The Death of the Queen is particularly according to the strictest rules of Justice; for she loses her life by the villainy of the very Person who had been the Cause of all her Crimes.—P. 48.

It was the tragedy as a whole in which these critics were interested, and Horatio's words lend them ample justification.   They knew less about psychology than more recent Hamlet critics, but they were nearer in spirit to Shakespeare's art; and, as they insisted on the importance of the effect of the whole rather than on the importance of the leading character, they were nearer, in their old-fashioned way, to the secret of dramatic art in general.

2

Such is the text—intrigue, fate, and blood—and what of the score? Others before me have remarked upon the melodramatic quality of the great tragedy, the abundance of sound and fury in it, of all that takes the

---

[2] *Allusion-Book,* ii, pp. 424-25.

eye, fills the ear, and shocks both;[3] and no one so shrewdly as the philosophical and literary critic Professor Bradley has noted the quantity of
noise required by the old stage-directions and implied in the play itself.
Cannon roar whenever the King takes a rouse, kettle-drum and trumpet
bray out the triumph of his pledge, and "Danish marches," "hautboys,"
and "flourishes" celebrate his movements. According to the unabridged
text of the last scene the cannon (robuster equivalent, as Mr. Bradley
observes, of our melodramatic pistol) should be kept booming continually,
—when Hamlet "gives a hit" and the King drinks to him, when Fortinbras
draws near on his march back from Poland, and when the body of the
irresolute dreamer is borne with a warrior's honors to the grave. "Go
bid the soldiers shoot," cries Fortinbras; whereupon, according to the Folio,
"a Peale of Ordenance are shot off." So it was at least in 1623;[4] but
never was it so when you or I have been at the theatre.

There is no irony intended,—none, as this cutting shows, that we today
are inclined to put up with, at any rate. Even in Shakespeare's day it
would have been considered barbarous if there were.[5] But it is thought
to be a triumph of Shakespeare's art that out of this sensational material
—"well-nigh every stimulant of popular excitement he could collect"—
he made the most mysterious and inward of his dramas. To my thinking,
and, if facts prove anything, to that of our modern producers as well, the
triumph would have been greater were the form better suited to the spirit.
The world does not move if the earth does, and harmony, not incongruity,
is the secret of art in the time of Shakespeare as in the time of Synge. "A
strange harmony of discords," says Mr. Bradley; but there is plenty of
that sort of thing in Elizabethan art without adding to it this incompre-
hensible variety.[6] It is easy thus oracularly to dispose of the matter,

[3] In recognizing this melodramatic element in *Hamlet* (as in all of Shakespeare's tragedies, indeed)
we do it no injustice. That in Shakespeare, as in the tragedy of the ancients, there is more of this than there
is in *Ghosts* or *Rosmersholm* no one can candidly deny. By the very distinction of the *genres*, then observed,
ancient and Renaissance tragedy was allotted the realm of terror and horror—"the mandates of kings,"
as the familiar phrase of Scaliger has it, "slaughters, despairs, executions, exiles, loss of parents, parricides,
incests, conflagrations, battles, loss of sight, tears, shrieks, lamentations, burials, epitaphs, and funeral
songs." That was the precept for Renaissance tragedy, founded on the practice of that time and earlier
times, and Elizabethan tragedy was, in so far, classical.

[4] Generally the entry of Fortinbras and his last words are omitted, the last cannon-shot, of course,
along with these. In the later prompt-books, such as Booth's and Irving's, cannon-shots are indicated only
twice—at the words the "King drinks" (or "Give me to drink") and at Osrick's "A hit!." Irving omits
the first, but requires a "shot within" to signalize the approach of the ambassadors.

[5] See above, p. 23.

[6] I cannot but think that Bulthaupt, an excellent critic too, and much after Mr. Bradley's own heart,
is franker: "Die tragische Färbung fehlt dem Schlusse ganz und gar, und es ist widerlich, ihn auf der
Bühne zu sehen, wenn uns die drei ersten Acte mit dem magischen Zwang ihrer Entwickelung gebannt,
wenn uns," etc. *Dramaturgie* (1894) ii, pp. 270-71. But before one condemns the close as inharmonious
had one not better consider whether it may not harmonize with a play a bit different from that which
one had conceived? It is in the same spirit that Bulthaupt (p. 325) complains of the inappropriateness of
Hamlet's being ready and fit to fight, and of his having "been in continual practice." This makes him too
businesslike and to the point; it shows that he is no weakling and intends revenge! It would have been
logical for Bulthaupt—but I am glad he refrained—to have recourse to Loening's interpretation—that
the practice is part of Hamlet's prescribed daily regimen. Like many other Germans, Loening thinks
the Prince sick in body as well as in soul. How foreign is either supposition to Shakespeare's art!

but one wonders how this harmony arises—or why to secure it the dramatist went so far afield.   In the sixteenth century, as in the twentieth, no great poet would have chosen to tell, or succeeded in telling, the subtle tale of a soul that criticism has thought to hear, athwart all this booming and trumpeting, and this mass of violent and bloody action in which man is pitted against man, Hamlet against Claudius, Polonius, Laertes, the pirates, Rosencrantz and Guildenstern, instead of an enemy seated in the depths of his bosom.   Shakespeare may have been in error, to be sure, led astray in the last scene in particular by his love of sensation, or his audience's love of it.   But the endings of his other plays are not like this, and there is no such noise and tumult at the death of Othello and Macbeth, who were warriors, or of Lear, who was a king.   Why should Shakespeare, in error, do here what he has not done elsewhere,—introduce repeated cannon shots at the close of this, presumably the most mysterious and inward of his dramas?   The dramatist could not have been thus led astray from habit or by his audience's expectations—still less could he have exerted himself so vigorously to lead his audience astray and defeat his purpose.   If there were such inwardness to the tragedy we may be sure that he would have had us suspect it: he would not have battered our ear-drums, instead.

But the dramatist is not thus in error if his drama be one—of character, to be sure, but of intrigue, fate, and blood.   If Hamlet was not an irresolute dreamer but an intrepid young prince who had fought off his enemies through the four acts, and now fell at the end of the fifth only after he had slain them all, then "the soldiers' music and the rites of war," which Fortinbras orders "for his passage," are but his due.   They are like a wreath or chaplet on his brow, from a soldier to a soldier, from the son of the conquered to the conqueror's son.[7]   Let them speak loudly for him, cries Fortinbras, for loudly a soldier salutes a soldier's grave.   Here is no irony, but pathos, rather, for Hamlet had not lived out even a warrior's years;[8]

[7] Hamlet was born, says the Gravedigger, the day that his father overcame the elder Fortinbras. This may, as Professor Schick says, be a circumstance not without significance.   It is only a casual remark, but Hamlet is frequently mentioned in connection with his father, and never with a slight upon the Prince.

[8] There can be no question about this, though exactly how young he is it is difficult to say.   Repeatedly he is called "young," or his "youth" is touched upon,—by Polonius, the Ghost, Ophelia, and the King.   (See the Concordance for these words and "young man.")   He is not so young, to be sure, as in Quarto 1; he does not call the King "father" as he does there (twice in III, ii) and in the *Fratricide Punished,* and no doubt did in the lost play.   Shakespeare's finished Hamlet is too reserved and dignified, too subtle and mature, for that.   And in Quarto 2 Shakespeare has added some touches, which by inference, at any rate, convey the impression of a somewhat greater age.   The Gravedigger says he went at his trade the day that our last King Hamlet overcame Fortinbras.   That, he says a bit later, was the day young Hamlet was born.   And finally he answers up, and tells the Prince that he has been sexton here, man and boy, thirty years.   Hence Hamlet must be thirty.   And that prepares us for another added touch in Quarto 2—when near the end the Queen says that Hamlet is "fat and scant of breath."   Both additions, together with the suppression of such details as I have mentioned in Quarto 1, may have been deliberately designed, as has been thought, either to make Hamlet mature enough for the reflections Shakespeare puts in his mouth or to fit the part for an older actor like Burbage.   But with the additions it is dubious.   As for the

but the main and prevailing note is that of tragic triumph. He was a pretty fighter, and this fight, says Fortinbras, was worthy of the field, and well has earned him a soldier's burial. There is on earth no end so fair, thought the Norseman, and Shakespeare and all England with him—then as now.

Thus there is nothing inappropriate in the artillery. And if a dramatist dealing with an heroic subject would not have put the like into his stage directions today, it is simply because "we have changed all that." We have no cannon just as we have generally no sound and fury, no fighting at funerals, no leaping into graves. But the shots fired when Hamlet gives his hits do not offend us when our hero appears to us sound and stalwart, and the scene—as story, not as psychology—is played for all it is worth. The shots make you hear what your eye may not be quick enough to see; the shots speak the language of the stage. Such portentous emphasis, to be sure, is not in our vein; but it is proper enough in a play in which there has been such violence of speech and demeanor in almost every act. And in this final scene of the revenge, toward which we have been impatiently looking, Shakespeare may well have felt warranted in scoring for full orchestra, and letting his thunders loose. This is the scene of scenes, where the energies of the Prince, checked and pent up throughout the play, are to be let loose. And if it was for such a brave and high occasion, not a weakling's desperate spasm, Shakespeare did not ill to call in the artillery. He may have made the error of over-emphasis, which he often makes—like a true Englishman, said Dryden long ago, "he knows not when to give over"—but he did not make the error, which he elsewhere never makes, of mistaking and defeating his own purpose. The great dramatist may overdo, but he does not do one thing

Gravedigger's remarks one wonders whether Shakespeare expected the audience to put two and two together in that fashion. What Shakespeare is interested in, and the audience too, is the humors of the Gravedigger and his concrete and circumstantial way of dating.

And as for "fat and scant of breath," those few words so precious to the pathologists, it is to me incredible that Shakespeare ever put the first of these into the text. That is not sound textual criticism, I know; but if ever an emendation seemed imperative it is here. "Hot" might easily have been so mistaken, (or to suit the actor it might deliberately have been replaced); and the advantage of such a word is not only that it does not clash with Hamlet's youthful elegance—"the glass of fashion and the mould of form"—"that unmatcht form and feature of blown youth"—and with his being in "continual practice" as a fencer; but also that it is in keeping with the King's words to Laertes as he arranges for the poisoned bowl—"when in your motion you are hot and dry" (IV, vii, 158. Cf. Quarto 1: "In all his heate," etc.; and *F.P.* IV, v; "wenn er erhitzt"). Besides, it fits better the occasion. One doesn't need his brows wiped if one be fat or scant of breath either, but one does if overheated. Or if one be really fat, why should it be noticed only here at the end? It is natural enough at this exciting moment for the Queen to remark upon a condition newly arisen, but not upon a permanent one. Her son is no fatter now than when he returned from his voyage, or (when we remember the actual shortness of the time involved) than he was at the beginning of the play. But the chief point is that the word "hot" keeps intact the dramatic situation as "fat" does not. At the word "hot" we are reminded of the King's words as he arranged for the bowl, and when the Queen invites Hamlet to drink we fear, for the space of four speeches, that he may. He had declined to drink with the King; now that he is hot he may, we fear, drink with the Queen. But his being overheated, it turns out, is the very cause of his refraining. "I dare not drink yet, madam; by and by"—"Come let me wipe thy face." If we have "hot," then, it is, fortunately, clearer that here again at the very end Hamlet is cleverer than the King—to the very end is more than a match for him.

thinking he is doing another. He does one thing, even to the point of calling in the artillery to make it clear; and it is the critics, far from the tumult and thunders of his theatre, who think he is doing another.

3

But what of our hero? In ridding him of his fault have we also robbed him of his charm? If not weak and erring, he is still unfortunate enough, unhappy enough, to be tragic. And all the individuality of his utterance and the poetry of his nature are left us—if not untouched, unspoiled. To what Hazlitt, Bradley, and Raleigh have in general to say of these no one will demur. Only the morbid psychology—the diseased spirit and limping will—is here denied him. His melancholy is not the melancholy of pessimism; his irony and cynicism are those of one who mourns his father, and his memory of a mother, not one who has lost his hold on life. At the end his interests are external, we have seen, but his soul is in them. Never before in the history of the world, I suppose, were words used so marvelously to show a man's changing moods as here—when he pardons Laertes, when he turns to his people, who loved him, to clear his name, when he wrests the cup out of Horatio's hand and prays him to live to clear it for him, and when he peers into the future for the news from England and to see Fortinbras seated on his father's throne. And I trust that not one quivering accent or hovering intonation of the verse need be lost to us if he be thought to speak in a manly strain. The pathos is simpler, that is all. His body is wounded but his spirit is whole, and he is not ready and glad to turn his face to the wall. Like a man he clings to his friends, is concerned for the welfare of the kingdom, but is concerned above all for his name and honor.[9] Like a man he struggles against death to tell his story himself, and wrests away the cup that his friend may live to tell it. "By heaven," he cries, "I'll have it!" The nineteenth-century Hamlet would not have had the strength or self-assertion to do that, or say that; he would not have had even the desire. "This trivial game of life,"[10] which he is presumed to despise, how much, even at his last gasp, he seems to care for it all! And by this interpretation, which we have been presenting, Hamlet's most famous utterance gains more, perhaps, than it loses.

> O good Horatio, what a wounded name,
> Things standing thus unknown, shall live behind me!
> If ever thou didst hold me in thy heart,
> Absent thee from felicity awhile
> And in this harsh world draw thy breath in pain
> To tell my story.

[9] These things men nowadays would not hold dearest of all, but an Elizabethan would.

[10] See Mr. Yeats's *Ideas of Good and Evil* (London, 1907), p. 162. For a century and more *Hamlet* criticism has been the vehicle of men's melancholy and pessimism.

There is less point, to be sure, to the words "in this harsh world draw thy breath in pain." The frail and shrinking spirit of the accepted Hamlet had found the world harsher than has ours. But why should *he* have his story told, or have Horatio draw his breath in pain to tell it? If all of it were to be told, surely he himself had rather draw the veil—had rather let Horatio drain the cup. But for our Hamlet the story is only not long enough, and he yearns to live a bit longer in the telling of it by his friend. He is a lord of the Renaissance and loves name and fame. He dies young, dies in the moment of his triumph, dies, as it must seem to others, with all this blood on his head. This is his triple tragedy, as Shakespeare, I think, intended it,—a simpler and nobler, possibly less interesting and piquant, conception than the usual one, though one not less appealing. To some it may even be more interesting because it seems to be more nearly what Shakespeare intended—more like him and his age.

CHAPTER VI

CONCLUSION

1

Enough, I hope, has been said to show what, as it seems to me, Shakespeare had in mind while, with devious and supple pen, he rewrote the old Senecan melodrama for the Lord Chamberlain's Servants. Like the thorough playwright that he was, he was interested mainly in the effectiveness of his play as a whole, not mainly in the character of the hero. He strengthened the structure, he sharpened the suspense, and in particular he pitted against Hamlet a King that was more nearly a match for him. And he elevated the character not only of Hamlet but of the King and Queen. But the problem was the motiving of the delay. By the hero's self-reproaches neither Kyd nor Shakespeare really explained the delay, for neither really motived it, that is, grounded it in character. Shakespeare's Hamlet, certainly, in reproaching himself, exhorts himself, in effect exculpates himself—he cannot lay his finger on the fault and he mends his ways. The sins of omission with which he charges himself are not to be reckoned against him any more than the like are to be in Seneca or Kyd. They are part of the story rather than of the character. And in general. Shakespeare deftly avoids or suppresses pretty much everything that would reflect upon the hero or put squarely before us the duty undone. No one reproaches him but Hamlet himself; on the other hand, everybody praises, honors, and fears him. Above all, in his rôle of revenger he is kept aloof and reticent. He has no confederates, he imparts no confidences to any one but Horatio (and those mainly off the stage) and he makes and discusses no plans. His saying so little about revenge leads us, at the theatre at least, to forget his doing so little about it; while he does other things and turns the King's game against him to the end. But his aloofness and reticence do not mean evasion, and he does not shuffle or deceive himself. From all this it appears that Shakespeare, having inherited a plot in which the revenge must be deferred throughout the drama, and finding it neither in his heart nor in the heart of his audience to have a revenger who would by nature so defer it, has shifted the revenge into the background, slurred over the delay, and by every means exalted and endeared to us the revenger himself. By all the cajoleries and enchantments of his art he has obscured and eluded the problem—not solved it. But drama is art, not psychology, and that the problem was unsolved was not recognized, it seems, till long afterward. In artistically obscuring and eluding the problem in his day did not Shakespeare, then, really solve it? Art is largely relative: it is for a time and a place, as well as for all times and places. It is an accommodation of one's thought not only to the particular medium one is using, but to the particular spirit and temper of the age. An irresolute and vacillating hero would in this case have been unacceptable; and if Shakespeare had solved the problem in so far as it was one in psychology, he would have left it unsolved in so far as it was one in art.

2

Yet it is not all so simple as that. There remains a good deal of obscurity and contradiction that cannot so readily be accounted for on the score of artistic reticence and finesse, or as the slurring and scumbling over of difficulties in a plot which could not easily be changed. Some of the confusion arises from there being two texts[1] and yet no text;—three ill-printed playbooks, and none of them a version on which the dramatist could have put his stamp. Still more of it is due to the fact that underneath all these lies the old play. The two revisions were not carried through evenly and consistently, and the old play and the earlier revision jut out through the last. But there is inconsistency that even this will not account for. There are contradictions in detail which arise from haste and carelessness; there is obscurity as regards the motives and relations of the characters, which arises from an indifference to the questionings of a spectator who should be also a thinker or reader—if indeed Shakespeare ever thought of a reader at all. There is the contradiction between Hamlet's two accounts of the reason for his affront to Laertes, on the one hand; there is the utter failure to clear up Hamlet's relation to Ophelia, on the other. Much of what I have just said may almost equally well be said of other plays of Shakespeare's, especially of *King Lear;* but it is true in a special sense of *Hamlet.*[2] Indeed, in the wildest of all vagaries of critical enthusiasm, the obscurity of the play has been made out to be one of its superlative virtues.[3]

---

[1] Three, of course, with the Folio.—For this confusion see above, p. 30.

[2] See the discussion of inconsistencies in both plays in Professor Bradley's *Shakespearean Tragedy*, text, notes, and appendices. In both cases Shakespeare was revising old plays; but Shakespeare's revision, here or elsewhere, does not mean the elimination of inconsistencies. His revision was creative, not corrective. He breathed into the old plays the breath of life; and while he raised the drama to a higher level of art, he worked so rapidly and carelessly that often, as in these two plays, he brought about more inconsistencies than were there before.

[3] I refer to the theory reproduced in Professor Wright's essay in the Columbia *Shakespearean Studies* (1916), cited above. It is really the old notion of Maurice Morgann that Shakespeare's characters are to be treated not as dramatic but historic personages, and that you know them as you know your friends. This confusion of the fictive and the real ought to have been disposed of by Mr. A. B. Walkley in his bantering and incisive essay on *Mr. Bradley's Hamlet* in *Drama and Life* (1907). See also my *Othello* (1915), p. 67, note 2. There is also in Mr. Wright's essay another sort of confusion—that of modern psychological characterization with characterization in the Middle Ages and Renaissance. · There is little in common between Hamlet's "I do not know why yet I live to say," etc., and the lapses of Cressida and George Meredith's Diana. For Hamlet's "I do not know" see above, p. 20, note 14. As for Cressida she is false to the religion of love; and though Chaucer condones it and makes her temptations plausible and her fall gradual, that is all there is to it. Only in Diana is there any of the mystery, the natural inconsistency and subconscious treason, that Professor Wright finds in all three. Only Diana really belongs to the world of Balzac, De Maupassant, Hardy, or the great Russians,—the world, indeed, of Mr. Wright and us all.

What troubles us now, however, is not the inconsistency in general but the points at which the play does not fit our theory. Although we have denied that Hamlet is a pathological or even a psychological character, there are, here and there, approaches to psychology and what may at least seem a psychological motivation. Hamlet is melancholy, for instance. The Elizabethan "humor" of melancholy, in other words, predominates in his temperament. He himself recognizes this in what he says concerning his condition to Rosencrantz and Guildenstern,[4] and the King once speaks of it too. And by several critics, such as Kuno Fischer and Professor Bradley, melancholy is made to explain his irresolution or disinclination to act.[5] But unless the dramatist had been more explicit this could not have been understood.[6]

For there is no necessary or frequent connection between Elizabethan melancholy and procrastination. It is not to be found in any other melancholy character on the Elizabethan stage—not in Marston's Malevole or Shakespeare's own Jaques, Don John, or Antonio, Merchant of Venice. Still less is there a necessary connection between melancholy and procrastination in one particular business, accompanied with zeal and promptitude in every other, as in Hamlet's case. There is no reason to accept such motivation as psychologically valid had Shakespeare indicated it—still less, to think he indicated it. Neither in his last soliloquy, where Hamlet fully considers the possible reasons for his failing to do the deed and dismisses them, nor any where else does he speak of this. It is impossible that Shakespeare should have let him thus consider the reasons, and leave the real one out. His business and purpose, we have seen, was to enlighten the audience, not baffle it. Besides, though recognized as a disease, melancholy is also a mood, a passion; and, arising, as it does in Hamlet, from a definite cause—his grief for his father's death and his mother's shame—it does not necessarily imply a pathological condition. He does not become less heroic because of it.[7] As described by him to Rosencrantz and Guildenstern, it furnishes the principle and groundwork scheme on which are portrayed Hamlet's gloom and thoughts of suicide, his irritability and fits and starts of emotion, his collapses into apathy or

---

[4] II, ii, 306 ff.: "I have of late, but wherefore I know not—lost all my mirth," etc. In this description Hamlet has given the symptoms, but the word melancholy he does not use. As I showed, however, in my article "Shakespeare, Marston, and the Malcontent Type" (*Modern Philology*, Jan., 1906), the Elizabethan audience would at once recognize and identify Hamlet's distemper. Since then I have observed that both Warburton in his edition of Shakespeare and Pilon in his *Essay on the Character of Hamlet*, etc. (*v. supra*), p. 15, recognize the symptoms too. In the eighteenth century the theory of the humours was still current.

[5] Loening, in 1893; Kuno Fischer, in 1896; Hans Laehr, in 1898; Professor Bradley, in 1904.

[6] Hamlet himself uses the word melancholy but once (II, ii, 630), to explain the illusion of the Ghost; the King is the only other person to use it (III, i, 173) and he does so without any necessarily technical significance.

[7] Hieronimo, Malevole, and many others were melancholy and retained their heroic character.

indifference after excitement—after rage, grief, or glee. And to that should be added the rôle which Hamlet plays of critic and cynic, who, like Marston's Malcontent, Malevole, holds forth on the theme that all is vanity, as in the churchyard; and bitterly amuses himself by launching shafts of irony at a criminal like the King, and by mocking and jeering at a ninny like Osric and a self-important dotard like Polonius.[8]

Whether Hamlet's fits of merriment and boisterous behaviour after the Ghost's disappearance, and after the play-within-the-play, are due to his melancholy or to the example of the Malcontent or the old Hamlet, we cannot say. In any case, both Marston's Malevole and his Antonio act somewhat like Hamlet in similar circumstances,[9] as does Tourneur's Vendice; but Marston draws his inspiration from Kyd, as Tourneur seems to do from Marston. In two cases, however, where outbursts of passion are followed by fits of dejection, there may seem to be approaches to the psychological, meant to exhibit how, when Hamlet explodes, he collapses. His passion with Laertes at the grave is one of these. But it is likely that this situation is fashioned in imitation of Antonio when he starts up and calls Pandulpho a liar for saying, as he mourns over the body of Feliche, that he is "the miserablest soul that breathes";[10] or else both situations, Marston's and Shakespeare's alike, go back to a similar situation in the old *Hamlet* of Kyd. And the simplest explanation for all of them, if we need to seek one beyond the demand for a stage sensation, is furnished in the description of the melancholy ones by Burton:

> And though they laugh many times, and seem to be extraordinary merry (as they will by fits), yet extreme lumpish again in an instant, dull, and heavy:[11]

The last words that he utters in the first of these fits of depression, after the disappearance of the Ghost:

> The time is out of joint;—O cursed spite,
> That ever I was born to set it right—

are meant primarily to motive the delay in the story and prepare us for it. If they be meant also to indicate a real antipathy to the task of revenge, they contradict the spirit of Hamlet's words and deeds elsewhere. But not every word or act of the hero, as we have seen, means character, whether in ancient drama or epic or the drama of the Renaissance. We remember the lamentations of Orestes before the deed and the wailings of Electra, whether in the *Choephori* or in any other of the Orestean dramas of the Greeks; the wild outcries of the Sophoclean Hercules; the fears and apprehensions of the much-enduring Odysseus (and of Æneas too) at every

---

[8] See the article on the Malcontent cited above, p. 72, note 4.
[9] Cf. *Antonio's Revenge*, v, ii, 47-49, his glee at the prospects of revenge.
[10] *Antonio's Revenge*, iv, ii, 76 f.
[11] Shilleto ed., i, p. 447.

evil turn of fortune in the tale.   Like the tears of Romeo and the trepida-
tions of Macbeth, they seem today little befitting these heroes' manhood,
except as we bethink ourselves how they serve to mark and measure for
us the tragic situation.   And Hamlet is not at his manliest here; for the
moment he is supine like Antonio, and bemoans his fate like Romeo,
Troilus, and Antony.   A momentous task faces him; and he is sad and
dejected, like Orlando before the wrestling, like Romeo before he enters
the Capulets' house, and like Brutus as he talks with Portia on the morning
of Caesar's death.   He may be infected with the pessimism which Mr.
Bernard Shaw complains of in Shakespeare in general.   But it is, rather,
a matter of art.   Where in Shakespearean tragedy is there any one who,
in the spirit of Browning and our whole age, holds life to be a high adventure,
welcomes fortune's buffets, and—even out of his love of life—goes forth gaily
to meet his fate?   That, in the Renaissance—as in the ancient—tragedy of
terrors, would be to take from the hero's fate some of its terribleness.
Hamlet, to be tragic, must shrink a bit from his.

3

I have mentioned these difficulties because they stand in the way.
The result of this *Hamlet* essay, too, is largely negative: though our concern
has been not with the prevailing critical theories but with Shakespeare's
purpose and conception, what we have learned concerning his conception
is, for the most part, that it is not that of the critics.   The chief positive
result is that Hamlet is meant for an heroic, not a pathetic figure, and not
one who falters or who deceives himself.   But if we ourselves should not
have hit upon the dramatist's conception and purpose, surely to look to
the dramatist's purpose is the right and proper critical method.   Looking
to our own needs and purposes instead has made the history of *Hamlet*
criticism a blot on the intellectual record of the race.   Age after age, philosophy after philosophy, has taken the hero and made him her own.   First
Hamlet was a sentimental creature, in the hands of Mackenzie and Goethe.
He was a "man of feeling," suffered more than the sorrows of Werther,
and carried Garrick's white handkerchief to wipe his eyes.[12]   Then he
was a prey to reflection, in the hands of Coleridge, Schlegel, and Gervinus.
He was Coleridge over again, as Mr. Bradley says, and Kant and Hegel
had him in thrall.   Then he was a pessimist, in the hands of Hugo, Dowden,
Döring, Türck.   Schopenhauer had succeeded to the throne.   And latterly
he has fallen, as he was predestined to do, into the hands of the Mephisto-
phelian searcher and sifter of motives on the Danube.   In Freud's and
his followers' hands self-deceptions and unconscious fictions are no longer
episodic but chronic and continuous; and whatever else in Hamlet thus

---

[12] According to the contemporary accounts Garrick made much of this.

fails of explanation, it thus becomes clear as noonday why he says he does "not know."

In Germany, indeed, he has become a national figure, and has changed as the spirit of the people has changed. He is like the magic picture of superstition, and has grown pale or bright as the national fortunes frowned or smiled. In the days of the great Frederick he was acted as a conquering hero. Sixty or seventy years later, in the days of disunion and humiliation, Börne cried, "Hamlet is Germany," and Freiligrath in verse said it again. "But since Germania has become conscious of her true character," says Professor Schick, "and on land and water has shown her mailed fist, voices have been raised which again emphasize in Hamlet his noble and heroic qualities."[18] Such voices are those of Klein, Schipper, Werder, and the rest. And what of him in Germany now, we wonder, since her mood again has changed? Nor is it public and national sentiments alone that have overwhelmed Hamlet, but private and individual, professional and personal whims and hobbies, if we could stop to show it, as well, whether in Germany or in the world.

Even the historical critic cannot utterly escape from the spell and sway of these public and private interests and predilections. Look to his author's purpose and the spirit of the author's century as he will, he lives in his own century and breathes the same atmosphere as his fellows. He has read Browning and Ibsen; even in being historical he follows the bent of the age. But it is the "function of criticism" to look away, to do what one can to escape. And that not merely in order to enter into the spirit of the Elizabethans, the Middle Ages, or the Greeks. Really it is also in order to enter more fully and aware into the spirit of today. Only as we continually break loose from our moorings in the present can we explore the past. Only as we explore the past can we know and appreciate the present. Comparison, contrast, differentiation, are the basis of our understanding of anything; in childhood they are the beginning of it. And only as we see that Shakespeare is not Ibsen, can we begin to see clearly what Shakespeare and Ibsen are.

---

[18] *Jahrbuch,* xxxviii, (1902) p. xlvii.

APPENDIX
THE OLD *HAMLET* INFLUENCED BY EURIPIDES

It is, in all likelihood, no accident that there is so close a correspondence between the passage in *Hamlet* quoted above, p. 49 note 14, and the two in Euripides. Shakespeare had not Greek enough, so far as we know, to read Euripides; but Kyd, who had been a Merchant Taylors' boy, probably had. In default of it, such a classicist as he could have turned to one of the three Latin translations then available. At all events, the parallels between the Orestean dramas and *Hamlet* seem to have to do with the pre-Shakespearean version. Aside from the above mentioned, these are:

First, the character of Horatio (the equivalent of Pylades, the famous faithful friend for whom there is no model in Belleforest) who calls forth from Hamlet more ardent expressions of friendship than are elsewhere to be found in Shakespeare, and who in the end would fain die with Hamlet, just as Pylades would die with Orestes, not only in the play which bears that name (ll. 1069 ff.) but in the *Iphigeneia in Tauris* (ll. 675 ff.). Horatio, certainly, was in Kyd's play; the combined testimony of the *Spanish Tragedy* and the *Fratricide Punished* indicates it.

Second, the hero's remark to his faithful friend as he plans revenge: "Should you chance to find my dead body, let it be honourably buried." This is not in *Hamlet* as we have it but in the *Fratricide Punished*, II, v, when the hero is about to enter upon his undertaking of revenge. Therefore it was probably in Kyd. It is a classical sentiment, and it is not in Belleforest. It seems to be a reminiscence of Orestes' words when about to kill himself: "Do thou, Pylades, stand umpire to our bloody feat, and, when we both are dead [Orestes and his sister] lay out our bodies decently," etc.—*Orestes*, 1065 ff.

Third, the fact that the hero's father was slain unhousel'd, unanel'd, or (in pagan equivalent) without the due rites of religious burial (*Electra*, 298, 323 ff.). Much is made of this in *Hamlet*, as in the Greek Orestes plays, and again there is nothing of it in Belleforest. It is, as Professor Gilbert Murray says, almost the central horror of the whole story.

Fourth, there is the almost explicit allusion, not necessarily to any one play, but to the Orestean story in general, where the Ghost bids Hamlet not to taint his mind nor let his soul contrive against his mother aught; and when he himself says: "O heart, lose not thy nature, let me be cruel but not unnatural . . . I will speak daggers to her but use none."

Most of these parallels have been noted by others before me, but either as evidence of Shakespeare's knowledge of the classics or as evidence of "the great unconscious solidarity and continuity, lasting from age to age, among all the children of the poets." This is a mystery, and Professor Murray falls back upon it "because Æschylus and Euripides and Shakespeare are strikingly similar in certain parts which do not occur at all in Saxo," and because Shakespeare did not know the Greeks. But Professor Murray would not need thus to fall back upon it, or add another to our myths of summer and winter, if he recognized the fact that Kyd was, unlike Shakespeare, something of a linguist and a pedant, knew Latin, French, and Italian, and Greek, very probably, as well.